Tank Attack at Monte Cassino

Tank Attack at Monte Cassino

The Cavendish Road Operation, 1944

Jeffrey Plowman

Pen & Sword
MILITARY

First published in Great Britain in 2020 by
PEN & SWORD MILITARY
An imprint of Pen & Sword Books Ltd
Yorkshire – Philadelphia

Copyright © Jeffrey Plowman, 2020

ISBN 978-1-52676-490-4

The right of Jeffrey Plowman to be identified as the author of this work has been asserted by him in accordance with the Copyright, Designs and Patents Act 1988.

A CIP catalogue record for this book is available from the British Library.

All rights reserved. No part of this book may be reproduced or transmitted in any form or by any means, electronic or mechanical including photocopying, recording or by any information storage and retrieval system, without permission from the Publisher in writing.

Typeset by Concept, Huddersfield, West Yorkshire, HD4 5JL
Printed and bound in England by TJ International Ltd, Padstow, Cornwall

Pen & Sword Books Ltd incorporates the Imprints of Aviation, Atlas, Family History, Fiction, Maritime, Military, Discovery, Politics, History, Archaeology, Select, Wharncliffe Local History, Wharncliffe True Crime, Military Classics, Wharncliffe Transport, Leo Cooper, The Praetorian Press, Remember When, White Owl, Seaforth Publishing and Frontline Publishing.

For a complete list of Pen & Sword titles please contact
PEN & SWORD BOOKS LTD
47 Church Street, Barnsley, South Yorkshire, S70 2AS, England
E-mail: enquiries@pen-and-sword.co.uk
Website: www.pen-and-sword.co.uk
or
PEN & SWORD BOOKS
1950 Lawrence Rd, Havertown, PA 19083, USA
E-mail: uspen-and-sword@casematepublishers.com
Website: www.penandswordbooks.com

Contents

Acknowledgements vii
Introduction ix
Prologue 1

PART I: THE ROAD TO REVENGE
   1. The Soft Underbelly 7
   2. Stalemate at the Gate to the Liri Valley 13
   3. Operation Dickens 21
   4. Cavendish Road 25
   5. Revenge Force 39
   6. The Token Texan Tankers 45
   7. Tank Killers Turned Tank Men 51

PART II: THE EXECUTION OF REVENGE
   8. Bradman Begins 63
   9. Into the Mire 69
  10. A Change of Heart 77
  11. Cavalry Ride to Albaneta 87
  12. Endgame 119
  13. The Attack in Retrospect 127

PART III: ON THE TRAIL OF REVENGE TODAY
  14. A Visitor's Guide to Cavendish Road 133
      Via Orsaia-Fonnone to Cavendish Road 133
      Caira Village to Cavendish Road 135
      Cavendish Road to Madras Circus 137
      Madras Circus to Massa Albaneta 146

APPENDICES
    1. Operational Orders 159
    2. Revenge Force 167
    3. Casualties by Unit 169
    4. Citations and Awards 173
    5. Galloway's Letter to Crowder 179
    6. The Other Side of the Hill 181
Notes 185
Bibliography 189
Index 191

Acknowledgements

I am grateful to the following veterans for their help in the preparation of this book: Pat Barton, Frank Brice, Allan Coleman, Theo Dore, Geoffrey Duff, Werner Eggert, Bob Frettlohr, Len Gallagher, George Kaye, Ray McFarlane, Rex Miller, Jim Moodie, Karl Newedal, Gerhard Pohle, Tom Sherlock and Basil Wilkinson. I am also grateful for the help of the following individuals: Lee Archer, Peter Brown, Terry Brown, Ron Crosby, Michael Dore, Aaron Fox, Wojciech Gawrych, Daniele Guglielmi, Zbigniew Lalak, Kay de Lautour-Scott, Karel Margry, Brendon O'Carroll, Perry Rowe, Peter Scott, Malcolm Thomas and Pino Valente.

I am also grateful to the following organisations for access to their material: the Alexander Turnbull Library (NZ), Archives New Zealand, National Archives (UK), National Archives and Records Administration (USA) and the Polish Institute and Sikorski Museum (UK).

I am also grateful to Yvonne and my children Catie and Matthew for their perseverance and support throughout the course of my research for the book.

Introduction

To the Allied troops who reached the Liri valley in January 1944 the monastery on the summit of Monte Cassino was an imposing and intimidating sight. Its position gave it a commanding view over the surrounding terrain and, along with the Arunci mountain range across the valley, completely controlled the approach to the Liri valley. For the Allies it was unfortunate because this was the best approach to Rome, their goal for the summer of 1944. Thus, if they were going to achieve this, they would have to take these heights, by no means an easy task. For many years before the Second World War the Italian Staff Corps had cited Monte Cassino as an example of an impregnable position and used it in training exercises for their officers. Thus, when the Germans sought sites for defensive lines in Italy, incorporating Monte Cassino into what was to become the Gustav Line was a logical choice. Over the course of the next five months the Allies tried to break through this defensive line, sometimes making direct attacks on the monastery or the heights above it, but all their efforts failed.

One of the lesser-known aspects of the fighting for Monte Cassino was an attack made by a tank force behind the monastery during the Third Battle. Exactly why this attack took place is not clear. Lieutenant General Bernard Freyberg, commander of 2 New Zealand Division throughout the war (and at this stage the New Zealand Corps), held the view that it was merely a sideshow or diversion. While that may have been the original intention, the fact remains that the Cavendish Road attack, as it has generally come to be known, achieved far more than any other part of the entire Third Battle for Cassino. It was one of those 'left field' ideas that caught the Germans at a vulnerable spot when they least expected it. The attack nearly drove a wedge through this sector of the German Gustav Line in Italy. Had it succeeded it would have achieved more than was expected of it. Fred Majdalany in his book *Cassino: Portrait of a Battle* was of the view that Snakeshead Ridge along with Points 593 and 569 were the key to securing the monastery but that may have only been part of the story. Sometime earlier in the struggle for the Cassino Massif the Americans had secured Point 593 at the end of Snakeshead Ridge and were on the point of taking Colle Sant'Angelo. It was at this point in the fighting that the commander of this sector of the Gustav Line, General Fridolin von Senger und Etterlin, expressed the view that had the Allies been able to establish substantial forces there and in the vicinity of Massa Albaneta, the objective of the attack, then he would have been forced to give up the Gustav Line. His reasoning was that the Allies would have been in a position to bring counter-battery fire onto his artillery in the Liri valley. Under such circumstances he would have been forced to start withdrawing his guns further away and hence denying his forces around Monte Cassino the support they needed.

The fact is, however, that the Cavendish Road attack did not succeed. Worse, it was set in train without the carefully laid pre-conditions for its launch having been fulfilled. It was supposed to be coordinated with the main attack by the Gurkhas on the monastery but at the last minute, with the Gurkhas' attempt not even getting off the ground, it was launched anyway and without any close infantry support. As Freyberg was later to comment, it all happened the wrong way round! Just why has not been made clear in the many books on the subject.

To cover the subject fully, this book has been divided into three sections. Part I deals with the events leading up to the Third Battle of Cassino (readers familiar with this may wish to skip these chapters), the building of Cavendish Road, and the men and the machines involved. Part II covers the attack itself and what led Freyberg to launch after the main attack on the monastery had failed. Finally Part III offers a guide to visitors wishing to explore the road up to Massa Albaneta.

The Cassino Commonwealth War Cemetery.

The graves of Lieutenant Jack Hazlett and Lance Corporal George Sorich in Cassino Commonwealth War Cemetery. Both served with the New Zealand Armoured Corps and both were killed on 19 March 1944. (*Peter Scott*)

Prologue

Amberly
14.6.2002

I was in this action! You would like what I thought and what I saw.

I was Buck Renall's gunner and being the first to go into action.

There was a gap we had to go through, on the right was a German gun position we did that over, we then carried on to the 'Nunnery' did that over. We were told to move on which we did. We had not gone very far when I could hear bullets hitting the side of the turret.

Buck who had part of his head above the turret could not make this out. I said to him to keep his head down or he would get 'it'. He put his hand on my shoulder and said 'Frank we were told that we held all that side of the slope' which was covered in scrub. Next we moved on and could see the back of the Monastery.

There was a gap of about 20 yards and we could see Germans running across and down a steep hill. Just before this not 5 minutes when Buck fell on top of me. He had been shot through the head. From then on we couldn't do much as I was busy with holding Buck. We then had to retreat to our start point.

We seemed to be under mortar fire all the time.

We heard over the wireless that a fire had started on the back of a tank, I think it was Stuffy Hazlett's tank. He was told to put it out. That put that tank out of action and of course he was killed.

After getting Buck out on checking around we found that our radiator was leaking so that put us out of action.

It seems to me that this attack lacked support, no ground support. Some one called for smoke at one time I don't know where it went but never saw it. Yet we always carry smoke shells in our tank. We were not asked to use them.

> I am sorry I have rambled on so much but when I see people like Buck and Stuffy being killed for what?
>
> Our tank crew was Jack Blunden, driver; Jeff Blatchford, spare driver; Bill Rob, operator; Frank Brice, gunner and Buck Renall our officer.
>
> By the history book it seems that we had all these units but never saw them. All I saw was 1 killed Honey [tank] or Bren [carrier] which went in to get a marooned person.
> The unit was never explained to us 'why'.
>
> Perhaps I blame some one for this error of judgement but why not? They the people who were responsible for this action never had a clue as far as I was concerned.
>
> Sorry to of carried on but very Bitter to express my self in this way.
> Reg. No. 573350 F. Brice
> Regards. Have a good day.
> Frank Brice.

This was the letter, exactly as I received it, from Frank Brice in answer to my questions about his involvement in the Cavendish Road attack in March 1944. He would not allow me to interview him but at least he was willing to write it down. After all those years he was still deeply upset about what happened then, and he was not alone in that. On 30 May 2000, in reply to a letter from me, Pat Barton, commander of C Squadron, 20 NZ Armoured Regiment, wrote:

> I just want to say that the whole affair was a terrible disappointment, the whole affair was. We were told that the Indian Division was to attack the same morning. We went ahead on that understanding but about 1.00pm we were told they had not moved so we were withdrawn – after having lost several tanks – not to mention the crews – who were not replaceable. I have a note from the Indian Division commander – Galloway – he was just as sad as we were about the whole affair.

Jim Moodie expressed his opinion in an interview on 1 January 1999:

> The most frustrating situation you could be in. Good blokes getting bumped off. You got to where you were supposed to be and no support. So harking back to the desert as infantry enemy everywhere

and no tank support. The only tank support in the desert was British tank support. It was the reverse three or four years later at Cassino, you see and no infantry. The tanks happened to be Kiwi and the infantry. Through no fault of their own but the command [sent] no infantry. The thing I knew at the time but not alone, the 22 Motor Battalion was trained to take over the ground during an armoured tank attack, that's what motor battalions were all about. It consolidates and holds ground taken by tanks. 22 Battalion was trained in this respect. It was sitting on its tail (as the Yanks would say on its ass) way down in a gulley someway waiting to be called in some soldierly attack themselves but were not occupied at that time.

For people like Pat Barton and Jim Moodie the inability to provide infantry support for this attack was incomprehensible. Both had served in 20 NZ Battalion when it was an infantry unit in the Western Desert and had first-hand experience of what it was like to fight without adequate tank support. When the battalion was converted to armour, all saw it as their chance to provide their fellow New Zealand soldiers with the support they needed. For that reason those who took part in the Cavendish Road attack were all dismayed by what happened.

On the other side of the hill the Germans were also perplexed as to why these tanks were sent in without infantry support. Karl Newedal, a German paratrooper who was on Point 593 at the time of the attack, had for many years wondered the same thing, so much so that when he came to Cassino for the 50th anniversary of the battle he was anxious to meet anyone who had been with those tanks that day. Even though he succeeded and met Jim Moodie, he never got the answers he wanted; Jim was hardly in a position to provide them as he knew so little himself. This book is an attempt to resolve some of those questions.

PART ONE

THE ROAD TO REVENGE

Chapter 1

The Soft Underbelly

On the morning of 15 January 1944 the Americans took Monte Trocchio, from the summit of which the broad flat valley of the Liri river seemed to stretch for miles. After their hard slog up from the bay of Salerno it must have seemed as though they only had to cross the Gari river below them and the road to Rome was theirs. In fact the Allies had come up against the Gustav Line, a switch line of the Bernhardt Line that ran along the lower reaches of the Garigliano river to Monte Cassino. What they were soon to discover was that the Germans had put a lot of effort into developing the defences along this line because of the strategic importance of the Liri valley.

How the Allies got this far is another matter. The Americans in particular had not wanted to be drawn into a campaign in what the British Prime Minister, Winston Churchill, liked to term the 'soft underbelly of Europe'. They had always set their sights on the main goal of a cross-channel invasion of France from England to open the 'Second Front' (the First Front being the Russian Front). The trouble was, at the time the Americans entered the war they lacked the resources, both men and materiel, to do so. Instead they found themselves with little choice but to begin their venture into Europe in the Mediterranean theatre of operations, first in North Africa in November 1942 and then in the invasion of Sicily in July the following year. Neither of these operations was particularly desirable to the Americans but the latter did offer the opportunity of an alternative route into France, via Sardinia and Corsica.

However, fate intervened shortly after the invasion of Sicily, bringing a new and unexpected opportunity as the unstable regime of the Italian dictator Benito Mussolini collapsed. Lacking the commitment to continue the war, the new Italian government began secret negotiations with the Allies that ultimately led to an agreement for the Italian troops to lay down their arms. Having had their hand forced, the Americans reluctantly agreed to landings on the Italian mainland but only on the understanding that it would help tie down German forces in Italy and secure the

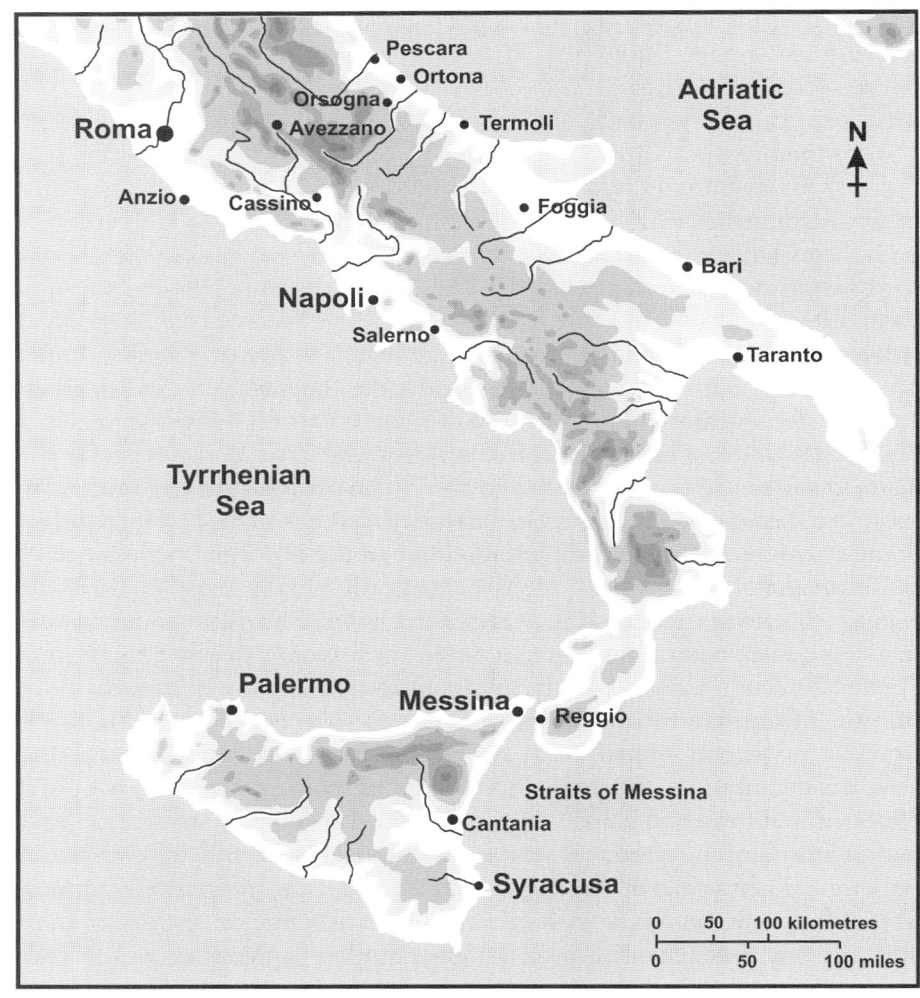

Sicily and Southern Italy

airfields around Foggia, from where they could target parts of mainland Europe with their long-range bombers.

The first landing was made by the British Eighth Army at Reggio di Calabria in the toe of the Italian peninsula but their progress was slow. This was soon followed by the main assault in the bay of Salerno by the US Fifth Army on 3 September 1943, this being conducted in conjunction with shipment of British airborne troops to Taranto. The main force at Salerno soon ran into trouble, the troops encountering bitter opposition as they fought their way off the beaches; at one point a German counter-attack threatened to throw them back into the sea. Ironically, more success was had on the Adriatic coast where the paratroopers, despite the lack of transport, heavy weapons and armour, managed to secure Bari and Brindisi before the area was sealed off by what troops the Germans had in the region. Eventually, the situation at Salerno stabilised and from that point on the Allies were free to advance. British troops entered Naples on 1 October, with Foggia on the Adriatic falling to paratroopers the same day. From there it was only a short hop to Termoli, the town falling a week after Foggia.

By now it was becoming apparent that the Germans were not going to give up Italy that easily. In fact Generalfeldmarschall Albert Kesselring, commander-in-chief of Heeresgruppe C, had been able to convince Adolf Hitler that a strong effort should be made to defend Italy south of Rome. Thus, even before the end of the battle for Salerno, Kesselring had set in motion the construction of a series of defensive lines across the peninsula, the first of which, the Victor Line, ran along the line of the Volturno river.

Unfortunately, the lack of a cohesive strategy among the Allies in the Mediterranean started to work against them. With winter fast approaching, the question arose as to what to do next. Given that their principal aims had been to eliminate Italy from the war and tie down the maximum number of German units there, the Allies had succeeded admirably in the first but the second was so vague as to be absolutely meaningless. Having seized the vital ports and airfields in the south of the peninsula, there was a feeling that they had gained enough territory to give their naval and air forces control of the southern Adriatic and Ionian seas. On the other hand, although pushing north would give them access to the airfields around Rome, they saw no advantage in areas beyond there. Nevertheless, their successes up to that point had given them hope that occupation up to the Alps was possible and that there might even be advantages to be gained by advancing beyond this range of mountains and into the plains of the Po river. At the Allies' Quadrant Conference in Quebec in August, there was general agreement that, while progress in Italy was likely to be slow, Rome, because of its airfields, was an important objective that should be seized as soon as possible.

At the strategic conference at Teheran at the end of November between Winston Churchill, Franklin D. Roosevelt and Josef Stalin, the Allies eventually agreed to a continuation of their involvement in Italy, despite misgivings on the part of Stalin that the Western Allies had designs on

Europe east of Italy. While their main focus was to be the opening of their Second Front in northwest Europe, they did agree to a landing in southern France, known as Operation Dragoon. This strengthened their desire to secure Rome and in fact to be well north of it by the spring of 1944 as Operation Dragoon required it to be launched from northern Italy. Thus, whether the Americans liked it or not, they were being drawn deeper into the mire that was the Italian campaign.

In the meantime all of this lay in the future. Right now what was critical to the security of Naples and Foggia was the need to secure a line along the Volturno and Biferno rivers. At the former the troops of the US Fifth Army, under General Mark W. Clark, came up against the Volturno river on 6 October, a day before the Eighth Army secured Termoli on the Biferno. From there on, General Sir Bernard Montgomery's Eighth Army ran into some tactically ugly terrain, where the plains around Foggia give way to hills cut by rivers running down to the sea.

Things were no better on the other side of the Apennines, where to the north of the Volturno river lay 40 miles of mountainous terrain, separating the Volturno from the Garigliano. Worse still, the autumn rains had struck in their full fury, turning the river flats into a sea of mud. In the end Clark's attack over the Volturno itself was not launched until the night of 12 October. With the river successfully crossed, the Germans were forced to retreat towards their next defensive position, the Barbara Line, which the Allies reached on 2 November. Soon this too had been breached, the Germans falling back to the Bernhardt Line.

The troops of the British Eighth Army, however, were forced to pause along the line of the Trigno river in order to regroup and reorganise their logistics thanks to the poor roads they had to operate over. They were not able to launch their attack until 2 November but a day later had penetrated 3 miles beyond it, leaving the Germans with no choice but to fall back to the line of the Sangro river. This the Eighth Army's forward elements reached on 9 November.

In the meantime, Clark's forces on the Tyrrhenian coast had reached the conclusion that north of the Barbara Line the only realistic route to the Liri valley ran through the Mignano Gap via Route 6, thanks to the marshy conditions on the coastal plain. The Fifth Army launched its assault on the mountains around Mignano Gap on 1 December, fighting continuing here until the end of the year when a blizzard forced the Americans to halt their attack to reorganise and replace their losses. Their final offensive to clear the Germans east of the Garigliano was launched on 4 January 1944, ending eleven days later after the Germans withdrew across the river.

From here the Allies' operational plans called for the Fifth Army to break into the western end of the German Winter Line at Cassino and drive up the Liri valley. At the same time, the Eighth Army on the Adriatic coast had been tasked with securing Pescara, from where it was to swing southwest along the route to Avezzano with the aim of threatening the German lines of communication. As part of this move, 2 New Zealand Division, which had entered the Italian campaign for the first time, launched an assault across the Sangro river on 18 November 1943. From there the Kiwis easily took the heights above the river but failed to secure the town of Orsogna on the next ridge, despite launching three assaults against it. Further east on the coast the Canadians reached the town of Ortona on 20 December, finally taking it after eight days of intense house-to-house fighting against its defenders. But by now the Eighth Army's offensive had ground to a halt, with little chance of it resuming until the spring.

Chapter 2

Stalemate at the Gate to the Liri Valley

By the end of December 1943 it had become apparent to the Allies that their operations on the Adriatic Coast had failed. If they were to get to Rome by June 1944, their only option was to concentrate their efforts on the Liri valley but there were constraints on this. One of their strategies for opening this door involved a seaborne landing behind German lines, codenamed Shingle, specifically in the Anzio-Nettuno area. This had to take place before the end of January 1944 as the landing craft and ships needed for it would have to be withdrawn in readiness for the landings in northern France. As a result of this, the Allied strategy around Cassino became slaved to the needs of Shingle. Prior to the launch of the operation the Axis troops had to be drawn south, and then the Allies would have to break through to the beleaguered troops around Anzio. Later the operations seemed simply to be driven by the desire to keep pressure on the German lines in the south so that they would not transfer troops further north.

The Germans were aware of at least some of the Allied plans. When it became apparent that Allied operations on the Adriatic had ground to a halt, they started to pull some of their formations out of the line, starting with 26.Panzer-Division. In addition, they placed their strongest defences at the mouth of the Liri valley. Here, the Allies were now facing the Gustav Line, a string of defences that coincided with the Bernhardt Line along the lower reaches of the Garigliano but which turned northwards through the Arunci Mountains before passing through Monte Cassino itself.

What then developed, from the Allied point of view, was a series of piecemeal operations, initially driven by the timing with which the troops closed up on the Garigliano and Gari rivers. The first assault on these defences, known as Operation Panther, was launched by the British X Corps over the lower Garigliano river on the night of 17/18 January

1944. The idea was to draw troops south from Anzio before the seaborne assault there was launched. In this respect it succeeded admirably. Within a matter of days Kesselring had despatched elements of the Herman Göring Panzer Division and 29.Panzergrenadier-Division south, their timely intervention thwarting British attempts to break through to the Liri valley by way of the Ausonia defile.

Operation Panther was intended to reach its peak at around the time the Americans launched their attack over the Gari river. This attack was also supposed to be coordinated with another attack by the British 46 Division around the confluence of the Garigliano, Gari and Liri rivers on the night of 19/20 January. This was not what happened, however. That attack failed miserably. As it happened, the Germans had just opened the sluice gates of a dam further up the Liri valley, turning the river into a raging torrent. As a result very few men from 46 Division managed to cross the Garigliano and those who did were soon rounded up and taken prisoner. Much to the annoyance of the Americans, the British division made no further attempt to cross the river, despite remaining in the area for another three days.

One day later the Americans launched their attack over the lower Gari river both north and south of the town of Sant'Angelo in Theodice. In this assault hundreds of soldiers from 36 (Texan) Division managed to cross the river, only to be trapped on the other side after their footbridges were destroyed by shellfire. Attempts by their engineers to push over Bailey bridges for their tanks also came to naught under intensive fire from the Germans. Those Texans not killed in the subsequent fighting were rounded up by the Germans. In the end the division had nothing to show for it. A further attempt a day later south of Sant'Angelo also failed.

Further north at Anzio, matters were not going any better. Operation Shingle, launched on the night of 22 January, failed to achieve what it set out to do. Its success depended upon the speed with which the invasion force could break out of their bridgehead but this appreciation was not passed on to the commander of the force, Major General John P. Lucas. Though the landings themselves were unopposed and the troops had no trouble establishing a perimeter, Lucas failed to exploit this success. Instead, he put his efforts into consolidating his positions to prepare for the expected counter-attack. While he was doing this, Kesselring rushed every available unit to the area. Within three days three German divisions and elements of eight others had established a ring around the bridgehead, with their artillery having a clear view from the hills and mountains above it. Worse still, another five divisions were on their way. Lucas launched a two-pronged attack at the end of January, before the German reinforcements arrived, but by this time the Germans were in a strong position and no real progress was made by the Allies.

Back on the Gustav Line, the next attempt by Fifth Army was on Cassino itself. As a preliminary operation, Général Alphonse Juin, commander of the *Corps Expéditionnaire Français*, was ordered to secure Colle Abate, Colle Belvedere and the village of Terelle to the north of Cassino. Juin was not particularly happy about this as his forces had been trying to bypass Cassino completely in a drive towards Atina, but nevertheless they complied and on 25 January launched their attack. After some intense fighting they secured both Abate and Belvedere but then came under an intense series of counter-attacks. At one time they were even driven off the summit of Belvedere and cut off, some without food and water, for three days. By that stage, however, the Germans had shot their bolt and the French were able to consolidate their hold on both features.

The monastery of Monte Cassino, towering over the Rapido valley and the town of Cassino, was an imposing and intimidating sight to any potential attacker. (*NARA*)

The next move on the Gustav Line took place on the night of 24/25 January when the American 34 Division launched an attack on Cassino town. It did not go well at first. The attacking battalions were only able to advance to the dry riverbed of the Rapido, where they became pinned down by intense fire. Despite lacking tank support, they managed to push some men across the river but they were eventually forced to retreat. On 27 January another attempt was made and this time they managed to get four tanks across, as well as several companies of infantry. Unfortunately cooperation between them was practically non-existent and although the tanks did provide assistance, they were soon knocked out. The infantry held on a little longer and one company even managed to reach the summit of Point 213 that night but decided that the position would become untenable in the light of day and so pulled back across the river, followed by the other companies who mistakenly believed that a general retreat had been ordered.

The Americans renewed the assault two days later, but this time further north. The infantry crossed successfully but soon became pinned down. Lack of armoured support proved a problem again. Five tanks managed to cross the river but most were lost, victims of an assault gun on the other side, before it too was knocked out by the last surviving tank. All was not lost, however, as the supporting tank battalions managed to push another twenty-three tanks across by way of the dry riverbed of the Rapido and in a combined attack reached the base of the hills. The following day they took not only the two prominent peaks across the river but the village of Caira itself, thus opening up the possibility of a two-pronged assault, one on Cassino and the other over the Cassino Massif.

As it so happened, their attack on the town did not go well. The Germans had abandoned the area around the barracks as soon as the Americans drew close but when the Americans tried to enter the town on 2 February they were beaten back. Worse still, that night five tanks were lost when they drove into the town ahead of their infantry, three of them being captured by the Germans. The following day the Americans gained a foothold in the town but it took another eight days of hard fighting before they managed to secure the gaol and the area around it.

It was a different story above them. Working upwards through the mist from Caira on the morning of 1 February one battalion took the summit of Monte Castellone, while the other captured Colle Maiola. On renewing their assault two days later, some progress was made until the Germans

Aerial reconnaissance photograph of Cassino township, 26 November 1943. (*Geoffrey Duff*)

put in a strong counter-attack on Colle Maiola. On the following day the Germans came under significant pressure. Working along Snakeshead Ridge and down from Monte Castellone, the Americans almost took Colle Sant'Angelo and Point 593, a situation that drove German commander Generalleutnant Fridolin von Senger und Etterlin to seek permission to withdraw from the battlefield. On 5 February the Americans finally captured the strategically important Point 593 for the first time and held it despite repeated counter-attacks. The fighting for this strategic point continued over the next five days, the position changing hands several times, until it was finally retaken by the Germans on the night of 10/11 February. Further attempts to dislodge them from it proved unsuccessful, while the Germans also suffered heavily in their attempt to retake Monte Castellone.

It was at the height of the battle for Point 593 and Colle Sant'Angelo on 4 February that the first of the reinforcements for Clark's forces around Cassino arrived, this being 2 New Zealand Division. At this stage its role was more that of a *corps de chasse* for the breakthrough, if it ever came. However, the divisional commander, Lieutenant General Bernard Freyberg, was of the understanding that they were expected to take over the assault if the American one failed and that is what eventually happened. To achieve this he was given command of a larger formation, the New Zealand Corps, consisting of his own division, commanded by Brigadier Howard Kippenberger, Combat Command B of the US 1 Armored Division and 4 Indian Division under Major General Francis Tuker, which had just shifted over from the Adriatic. A fourth unit, the British 78 Division, was a later addition, its arrival being delayed by snow in the Apennines.

Freyberg launched his controversial attack on Monte Cassino on 15 February – controversial because of the bombing of the monastery. Not that the bombing made any difference in the end. Freyberg's attack initially followed a similar strategy to that of the Americans before him but this time with the major thrust initially being made along Snakeshead Ridge with the objective of securing Point 593. Once this had been achieved, they were to advance on the monastery, after which they were to descend and cut Route 6 in the valley below. It was at this point that 28 Maori Battalion was to launch an attack across the Rapido river, secure the railway station and, ultimately, link up with the Indians.

It was in the execution that things went badly wrong, not the least of which was the bombing of the monastery itself. The Indians were not informed of the exact day of the bombing until the last minute and it was too late to change their plans to attack Point 593. However, it made no difference. Their first attack and subsequent ones were not able to dislodge the hold the German paratroopers from 1.Fallschirmjäger-Division had on the summit, even when a second brigade of Indian troops was brought in on the night of 17/18 February. Moreover, with the tracks up to their positions on Snakeshead Ridge unable to support wheeled transport, they were forced to turn over their 11 Brigade to portering duties but this did not prove to be enough and the attack that night failed.

A further disaster was heaped on the New Zealand Corps that same night when the Maori Battalion launched its attack over the Rapido. Though the two companies sent across had some success, securing the railway engine shed (known as the Round House) and part of the station area, they were not able to capture a prominent hillock known as 'The

Stalemate at the Gate to the Liri Valley 19

Monte Cassino and its monastery were bombed at the behest of Lieutenant General Bernard Freyberg, commander of the New Zealand Corps, prior to the launch of the Second Battle of Cassino. (*George Kaye*)

The monastery suffered considerable damage as a result of the bombing, only the south-west wall surviving intact. In this view Point 435 (Hangman's Hill) is immediately to the right of it, while Rocca Ianula (Castle Hill) is between them and to the rear. (NARA)

Hummocks' to the south. Worse still, the New Zealand engineers, who had been detailed to repair a number of demolitions along the railway embankment, were unable to repair the last two, meaning that tanks could not be brought across in support. With their requests to withdraw denied, the Maori troops were forced to hold on throughout the morning of 18 February and into the afternoon, albeit covered by a heavy concentration of artillery smoke. In the end it all came unstuck. Using the cover of that same smokescreen some German troops, supported by two assault guns, launched a counter-attack that drove the Maori defenders out. Thus ended Freyberg's first attempt to take Monte Cassino.

Chapter 3

Operation Dickens

Freyberg's attack on Monte Cassino in February 1944 had no sooner died away than he was planning the next one. Whatever was happening at Anzio, he was under an obligation to maintain pressure on the Liri valley front, if for nothing else than to prevent the Germans switching reserves back to the north. Another driving force was the desire of the Allies to encourage the Germans to keep as many of their forces in Italy as possible before the launch of the cross-channel invasion of Normandy. The commander-in-chief of the Mediterranean theatre, Field Marshal Sir Harold Alexander, had also made it plain that if Freyberg did not do it, someone else would be found to undertake this venture. For his next attack, although elements of Freyberg's plan remained the same, he had decided to make his main effort through the town. The failure of the Indians to gain traction on the ridges above the monastery had convinced him that this option was not viable. The front for the attacking troops along Snakeshead Ridge had proved too narrow, allowing only a company-sized force, plus the Germans were able to bring fire onto the attackers from all manner of directions. They were also able to deploy additional troops in dead ground and caves and these they were able to use to quickly reinforce areas under attack.

For this attack the New Zealand Corps consisted of 2 New Zealand Division under the command of Brigadier 'Ike' Parkinson, 4 Indian Division now under Major General Alexander Galloway, the British 78 Division and Brigadier General Frank A. Allen Jr's Combat Command B of the US 1 Armored Division. It was hardly an adequate force for the job ahead but it was all that Alexander could spare as he was planning a larger offensive for the spring. The problem was that what Freyberg really needed was infantry but the NZ Corps was heavy in armour. Combat Command B, for instance, was a peculiar formation. Its Task Force A was made up of a tank destroyer battalion, an engineer battalion, two battalions of infantry and a recce company from one of 1 Armored Division's armoured infantry regiments. Task Force B, however, had only one company of engineers supporting two tank battalions, a tank destroyer battalion and an armoured reconnaissance company.[1] For the forthcoming battle Freyberg's plans included lending them some infantry. Although Freyberg could call on the infantry of 78 Division, the main assault was to be carried out his New Zealanders and Galloway's infantry largely because they were in place to carry out the operation. The problem there was 2 NZ Division was short on infantry itself, having been reconstituted as a mixed division while still in Egypt, with one of its three infantry brigades being converted to armour. Galloway's division was also short on infantry since February when it had been badly mauled in the assault on Monte Cassino.

For his new offensive Freyberg considered two options, a river crossing or house-to-house fighting in Cassino itself, though of the two he favoured the latter. The Fifth Army commander, General Mark W. Clark, was keen on another river crossing, something more like the attack by the Texans in January, apparently. Alexander, however, did not want to waste the New Zealand Corps in another fruitless attack and came down on the side of Freyberg. Thus, for his new plan Freyberg decided to launch the attack from the division's positions in the northern part of Cassino but only after the town had been given a thorough going over first. The option of entering the town from across the Rapido river along the axes of Route 6 and the railway embankment had been considered but thought to be too risky, especially after the experience of the Maori Battalion in the earlier attack. The ground, sodden with rain, offered no other options.

The new plan, codenamed Dickens, called for a side-by-side advance by the New Zealanders and the Indians, the former through the town and the latter on the hills above (*see* Appendix 1). Orders issued to 6 NZ Brigade on 23 February also included specific instructions for 4 Indian Division:

4 IND DIV is to:
 (i) assist ops of 2 NZ DIV[ISION] by neutralising enemy posns on eastern slopes of M. CASSINO with SA and mortar fire and by harassing enemy mov in CASSINO prior to zero.
 (ii) after capture Pt 193 (G 854213) take over and secure the feature.
 (iii) in conjunction with the adv of 2 NZ DIV[ISION], attack South.
 (iv) maintain pressure in sector N.W. of the MONASTERY to prevent the withdrawal of enemy reserves from that area.

Thus the two divisions would be able to provide mutual support for each other. In what was to be known as Phase Instep, there were two main objective lines for the New Zealand infantry. The first, Phaseline Quisling, ran along Route 6 as far as the Hotel Continental corner and then up to Point 193, otherwise known as Rocca Ianula or, to the Allies, Castle Hill.[2] Once secured, this was the cue for the Indians to take over here and be in a position to advance to the next stage in tandem with the New Zealanders. Part of the planning assumed that the Hotel des Roses would be captured early as Freyberg was hoping to send up some tanks to assist the Indian Division in securing their next objective. The second objective line was Phaseline Jockey. This was anchored at the railway station and a building known as the Baron's Palace, where Route 6 curved around Monte Cassino and into the Liri valley, the line itself projecting south towards the confluence of the Rapido and Gari rivers. During this phase the Indians were to secure the various turns in the serpentine road to the monastery, right up as far as Hangman's Hill (Point 435), so-named because the remains of the gantry of the old cable-car to the monastery looked like a hangman's gallows from below.

An intrinsic part of the operation was use of the air force in a tactical role to level the town in the belief that it would remove all opposition. This was to be followed by heavy artillery bombardment. Casualties from 'friendly fire' would be avoided by withdrawing the troops of both divisions from their forward positions for the duration of the bombardment. Freyberg was understandably concerned that the strongly constructed buildings in the town would offer good protection to the defenders and that precision bombing would be a way of overcoming this. Nevertheless, while air force officers were of the view that this was achievable, there were concerns from that quarter that infantry would only be able to advance with difficulty through the town and it would be impossible to get tanks through. Freyberg was dismissive of this viewpoint, advancing his opinion that if his armour could not get into the town, then neither could German tanks. He also felt that it ought to be possible to use bulldozers to clear the rubble afterwards. Thus, there seemed to be an expectation that the infantry would be able to advance through the remains of the town as if it were a standard operation in open country. The plans even talked about the attack in terms of a typical advance, with a lifting barrage advancing at the rate of 100 yards every 10 minutes. In fact the entire operation appeared to hinge upon the bombing and artillery bombardment leading to the total destruction of the German paratroopers in the town, thus facilitating a quick breakthrough by 6 NZ Brigade, with 5 NZ Brigade being held in reserve for the exploitation phase.

Once Jockey had been secured, Task Force B of Combat Command B was to lead the breakout into the Liri valley. Because this group was heavy in armour, Freyberg had attached 21 NZ Battalion to it. This force was to secure the next Phaseline, Libel. At this point Phase Cobra could begin, whereby 4 NZ Armoured Brigade was to strike south and take Pignataro and Sant'Angelo in Theodice, clearing the western bank of the Gari river in the process. This would see the execution of Phase Joiner, when 78 Division was to cross the river and link up with the New Zealand armour in a drive up the Liri valley, a move to be made in conjunction with Task Force A of Combat Command B. During this phase the Indians were to continue to support this with the rather vague instructions that they were to advance westwards and capture the monastery.[3]

One thing noticeable in these plans is that the monastery was not specifically named as an objective; instead the Indians were simply to support 2 NZ Division in its attack (Appendix 1), something that apparently annoyed Clark. In fact when shown these plans Clark was deeply shocked to learn that Freyberg would consider launching his exploitation up the Liri valley before capturing Monte Cassino. In Clark's opinion: 'It is absolutely impossible to mass for an attack down the Liri valley without first securing the commanding elevation on one flank or the other.'[4] According to his diary, two days after these discussions Freyberg came back with a modified plan which included an attack on the monastery.

Freyberg unveiled these plans at his Corps conference on 2 March.[5] Most noticeable was a move away from the side-by-side assault of the two divisions. Instead, after taking over Castle Hill from the New Zealanders, the Indians were to launch a phased assault on the Cassino massif, via Hangman's Hill and ultimately the monastery. Included in this was the proposal to use New Zealand armour to drive all the way up the serpentine road in the dark to assist the Gurkhas in securing this prize. Freyberg anticipated that this final assault would be launched around midnight. One point he did emphasise was that the capture of the monastery was entirely dependent for its success on the commencement of the armoured exploitation into the Liri valley. To achieve this, New Zealand engineers were supposed to have started bridging the Rapido and clearing mines on Route 6 shortly after the main assault force had reached Phaseline Jockey. Thus, perhaps the most significant change in Freyberg's plans, apart from putting the monastery firmly on the agenda, was an apparent decoupling of the New Zealand and Indian arms of the assault, the Indians no longer providing flank protection for the New Zealand attack.

Chapter 4

Cavendish Road

One serious issue that had faced 4 Indian Division during the February attacks was that of supply to their troops on Snakeshead Ridge and Colle Maiola. All of their munitions, food and other supplies had been brought up by porters and mules using rough, steep tracks carved into the side of the mountain. They had also found it necessary to reassign the fighting troops of their 11 Brigade to carry out these duties. One path that they had been using ran up the eastern side of the mountain from the vicinity of the old Italian barracks to Colle Maiola. As early as 16 February 12 Indian Field Company had started work on improving it to take mules and by 19 February it was complete. However, the previous day Lieutenant Colonel Edward Stenhouse, their Commander Royal Engineers, had decided to upgrade it to take jeeps and so the task was handed over to 4 Indian Field Company, who dubbed it 'Roorkee' Road.[1] They finally finished it at the end of the month.

Not far away in the Valle Pozzo Alvito was a peasant's foot-track some 2-feet wide that ran up from Caira to the basin below Colle Maiola. A branch track existed to provide two crossings over two nullahs (an Indian term for a dry watercourse) that crossed the track part way up. The upper track provided a better alignment but where it crossed the nullahs there was a sheer, 60-feet-long rock face. However, this was the one the Indians wanted to upgrade to take jeeps as it offered a better overall gradient, even though more serious work was required to get it past the nullahs. This upper track was christened Cavendish Road by Stenhouse after the name of the road in Bournemouth in which his father lived. The initial idea was for the Indian engineers to develop this track to take mules, with the provision that later it could be widened to take jeeps. On 17 February 4 Indian Field Company was ordered to commence work on the lower track, widening it to 4 feet to enable it to take mules, while work on the rest of the track, including the upper portion through the rock face, converted to take jeeps.[2]

26 *Tank Attack at Monte Cassino*

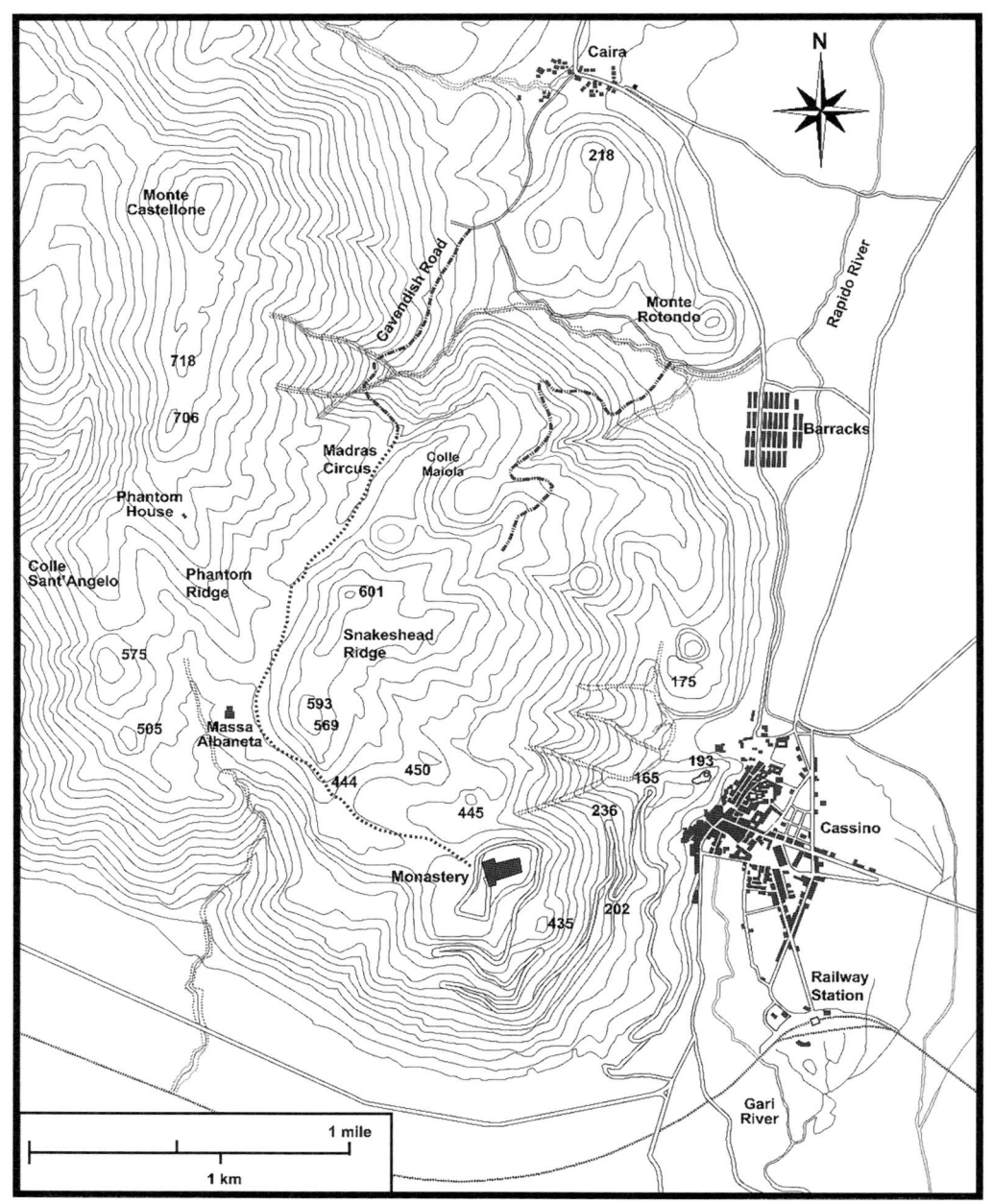

Monte Cassino, showing the route taken by the tanks to Massa Albaneta from Caira via Cavendish Road.

A signpost somewhere on Cavendish Road, the red eagle insignia on the signpost acknowledging that it was constructed by units from 4 Indian Division.
(*Polish Institute and Sikorski Museum*)

This jeep is on the lower reaches of Cavendish Road, heading towards the first of the two dry watercourses or nullahs that crossed the track. (*Polish Institute and Sikorski Museum*)

The issue of the track, particularly, must have been of concern to the Indians, as on 21 February the Indians invited Colonel Frederick Hanson, the New Zealand Division CE NZ Corps, to inspect the work on Cavendish Road. One of Hanson's recommendations was that a bulldozer might be of use on the lower portion of the track, and he arranged to send one over to them. Hanson also recommended that the upper portion of the track should be camouflaged where it came into view from Monte Cairo. Unfortunately, at that point the weather turned against the Indian engineers. On 23 February it rained all day and although the camouflage netting and poles arrived that evening, they could not be erected until the following night. Despite this a D4 bulldozer, which had arrived overnight, had managed to start work and by 25 February had shifted stone and rock that had not previously been thought to be achievable.

Nevertheless, it would appear that the visit had given Hanson some food for thought. Thus on 27 February Stenhouse and some of his engineers paid another visit to Cavendish Road. Accompanying them were some New Zealand Armoured Corps personnel,[3] Lieutenant Ron Griggs and Sergeant Frank Milne from 19 NZ Armoured Regiment. Though primarily there to inspect progress on the road, they had also been tasked with reconnoitring another possible route for tanks up to the top of Monte Castellone and then down through the French sector. Two days later they put forward their recommendation that the Indians expand Cavendish Road from an 8-foot cut to a 12-foot cut to take tanks up to the capacity of a Sherman. They also proposed realigning the track near the top, extending it out a further 150 yards in order to get over the need for a hairpin bend. Approval to widen the road to take tanks was given on 29 February and work commenced on 1 March, with the aim of completing it in fourteen days. This coincided with another period of rain, though Cavendish Road stood up rather well under this, despite the water pouring over it from the hills above. The only damage caused was the collapse of some walls on the unfinished portion.

To assist the Indians, Hanson loaned them 2 Platoon, 6 NZ Field Company, under Second Lieutenant Thomas Higginson, two D6 bulldozers, two Worthington trailer compressors and crews to operate them, all under the command of Captain Colin Hornig. They moved up to the area around the Barracks on the night of 2/3 March, by which time the road had been widened far enough to allow the trailer compressors up as far as the nullahs, where they were to carry out the blasting. The following day the D6 bulldozers were driven up to Cavendish Road but only got as far

This jeep was photographed on the section of Cavendish Road between the first and second nullahs. This area, hidden from enemy observation, was used for storage of ammunition, in this case mortar rounds. (*Polish Institute and Sikorski Museum*)

Looking up the ravine of the second nullah that crossed the road. A culvert and stonework were required to get the road around the sharp bend and across the dry waterbed.
(*Polish Institute and Sikorski Museum*)

as the tunnel camouflage netting because it was too small to allow them to pass through (or for that matter the Sherman tanks that were supposed to use the road later). There was nothing left to do but leave them at the tunnel until it could be widened. Some men from 21 Indian Field Company started work on this immediately, the idea being to move the nets at dusk. Luckily for them, mist descended on the road around 1430hrs, allowing them to complete the job that afternoon.

From that point on, work on the road was divided up with the NZ Corps engineers working on the part of the road from the camouflage netting to just short of the nullah, and 21 Indian Field Company focusing on the rocky portion of the road on both sides of the nullah. The upper portion of the road up to a bowl just below Colle Maiola became the responsibility of 4 and 12 Indian Field Companies, with 21 Indian Field Company at the top, and for that reason was dubbed Madras Circus.

Lieutenant C.J. Matthews from 6 NZ Field Company recalled later their arrival at the work face on Cavendish Road:

> Three field companies from 4 Indian Division had been working on the track for some time and had completed about half of it. They had only one D4 dozer and two compressors; almost half their work had been done by hand with crowbars, picks and shovels. We thought when we arrived that the job would take weeks. It seemed a hell of an undertaking as the route led up to what was almost a cliff face. Here the Indian sappers were working like monkeys, loosening rocks and laboriously shifting them away. They would never get through. The assignment was both dangerous and spectacular, for the whole area was within easy enemy range, while the bivvies were so close to the Indian guns that sleep was impossible while they were in action. Enemy posts looked straight into parts of Cavendish Road which, like Duncan's road at Orsogna, was shielded from view by camouflage netting, a precaution that seemed to annoy the would-be spectators.[4]

Matthews and his men were forced to move from their first campsite:

> We shifted out of our quarters after it was shelled at 0300 hours one night. After that we lived on the flat about 2 miles away, coming in by armoured car before first light, leaving the vehicle under cover in a creek, and going out again after last light. It was a fairly long day.[5]

Starting around 3 March the Indians were forced to use picks and shovels to remove loose earth and stone from around rocks and dig out shale.

The second nullah was out of direct enemy observation and thus was an important resting-up point. Nevertheless, camouflage nets appear to have been erected over some sandbagged emplacements. (*Polish Institute and Sikorski Museum*)

Jeeps working their way up and down the road above the second nullah. (*Polish Institute and Sikorski Museum*)

34 Tank Attack at Monte Cassino

Crowbars were then used to remove boulders around 2–3 feet in diameter, while Bailey jacks could take out boulders up to 5 feet in diameter. When these had been dislodged, they were broken up with sledgehammers. Hand-placed charges were then used with great success against pinnacles and weathering rock. Once the solid rock face was reached on 6 March it was possible to start drilling boreholes for charges and start some serious blasting. However, the problem there lay with the compressors they had taken up. A total of seven were available but only five of them worked. By 5 March two of them had broken down. The one with 4 Indian Field Company failed and was sent down for repair that day. The clutch on the one with 21 Indian Field Company also failed but when another was sent up it fell over the side of the road. Two days later it was still stuck up at the top and unable to work so the New Zealanders sent up one of theirs.

As Matthews later related:

> So in our combined work they went ahead making a rough track. We came along with compressors, did the demolitions and then used our

A general view of Cavendish Road in late May 1944, taken from above the two nullahs. The start of the lower mule track, where it led off the main road, can be seen to the right. (*Polish Institute and Sikorski Museum*)

bulldozers. All day long the Germans sent over shells and mortar bombs. They were very close in the valley over the ridge above the Caira village. Here it was possible to hear the mortars fire and then wait for the descending bomb. They had a clear view of what we were doing from the sector they held in the mountains to the northeast. Therefore the Indians camouflaged the track, lugging up 10-foot poles, digging in and propping them up with stones on the lower edge, and placing overhead poles across the hillside. On this framework they put camouflage nets.

Our work was in regular stages – drilling for a day and a half, then blowing and then bulldozing for two or three days. We worked in conjunction with the Indians, more or less give and take. If there was a hold-up we could get the Indians to give a hand and clear the way.

They did most of their work by hand and the amount they did surprised us. There was a lot of 'nattering' and individuals seemed to work very slowly but in the end the amount each group did was very substantial. It was just steady work by a lot of men. They certainly stuck to it. Their cookhouses and bivvies were in some dead ground. Some slept in crannies and clefts in the rock up the hillsides.[6]

Walter Kerse, from 2 Platoon under Second Lieutenant Tom Higginson, explained what work they did:

We supervised the boring and the placing of explosive, the use of instantaneous fuse. We laid that out in long strips and short stretches down to the explosives with the detonators. And the instantaneous fuse was connected to a slow burning fuse and we cleared everybody out of the road and just let the blast go. And then as immediately as that was done we then proceeded to drill another lot of holes. We worked on that road, I suppose, about four or five or six nights. The nights were worse than the daytime because although we were never shelled doing the road the Indians suffered casualties, we didn't. We had a terrible time at night with the rocks rolling down the side of the hill and crashing through the undergrowth and low scrub. Once we had reached the part of the road where the rock [that] was very, very solid, almost marble, ran out, we withdrew.[7]

From time to time the Germans shelled the area too. On 25 February 21 Indian Field Company was shelled, with one man killed and another wounded. On 3 March another shell fell in their company area, killing

Jeeps line the final stretch of Cavendish Road up to Madras Circus. It was around here that the M5A1 Light Tanks were forced to lay up while waiting for the order to launch Operation Revenge. (*Polish Institute and Sikorski Museum*)

four and wounding five others. Three days later Captain Bruce Hornig was killed, as Kerse related:

> When we came back on the second day we were having a drink around a cup of coffee when we were very heavily mortared and shelled. Most of the shells over-carried onto the flats beyond. But the Nebelwerfers, six-barrelled mortars, were landing some of them in the low scrub on the very steep side of the sharp hill above us. We were protected by the hill except for where those shorts landed; they started rocks rolling, which crashed down through the [scrub]. After we'd had a cup of tea, and unbeknown to us, Bruce Hornig was actually at his bivvy, which he had established that morning while we were working. And when I was going back up to where my slit trench was dug into the side of the hill he was lying dead beside his ablution bucket. He had been having a shave and clean up and he didn't have a mark on him. I gather that one of the Nebelwerfers had burst above him and he was just killed by the blast.[8]

In the meantime the Indians were able to speed up work on the track by carefully monitoring the process and shifting their sappers around to where they were needed. Work on the road was finally completed on the night of 10/11 March but not before a misunderstanding had to be sorted out. While Stenhouse and Galloway were being shown around on 9 March, Galloway was a little upset to discover that the New Zealand engineers had been ordered to work all night in order to have the road ready the next day. With memories of the confusion following the bombing of the monastery during the previous month, and fearing there were plans to use the road before 11 March, he sought (and received) assurance from Hanson that no such plans existed.[9]

With Cavendish Road complete, Freyberg now had the option of doing something the Germans least expected: sending a force of tanks up behind the monastery. This new operation, codenamed Revenge, became the responsibility of 7 Indian Brigade and was to be executed by their reconnaissance squadron under the command of Major Malcolm Cruickshank, with Company D, US 760 Tank Battalion, under the command of Lieutenant Herman R. Crowder, in close support.[10] The aim of the attack was to advance towards Massa Albaneta with the view to disrupting the Germans in that general area and, if the situation permitted, to exploit southwest towards the monastery. Though purely a tank force, there was provision for reinforcing it with a company of infantry from 1 Sussex Regiment.

In the words of an American combat report, the general idea was to 'spread chaos and consternation in the ranks of the enemy'.[11] In addition, though not part of Revenge, there was a proposal for 1/2 Gurkhas to send a company along Snakeshead Ridge in the event that the enemy showed signs of breaking up. The critical part of the plan was that it was not to be launched until after the successful capture of the monastery by the Indians and the cutting of Route 6 south of Cassino by New Zealand armour.[12]

Chapter 5

Revenge Force

As set out in the original orders, Revenge Force was made up of two units: 7 Indian Brigade Reconnaissance Squadron and Company D from the US 760 Tank Battalion. Of the two, less is known about the Indian unit, apart from the fact that at the time of the attack it was commanded by Major Malcolm Cruickshank and took into battle three Shermans and five recce tanks, though whether this was the entire unit is not clear (*see* Appendix 2).[1]

Likewise, the particular model of Sherman issued to the Indians is also unknown, though most probably it was the Sherman III (American designation: M4A2 Medium Tank). Their recce tank, however, was based on the Stuart III (American designation: M3A3 Light Tank). The Stuart III was in essence a Stuart I or II with a new hull and enlarged turret. Gone were the heavy hatches in front of the driver's and co-driver's stations, the former only capable of being opened by the driver with difficulty. Also gone was the hatch in the glacis plate that could only be opened from the outside; this was the only way to free the driver in emergencies in the Stuart II because there was no way he could escape, especially once a turret basket had been incorporated into the design. The hull of the Stuart III now had sloping sides and a sloping glacis plate, replacing the box-like structure of the Stuart I and II, this adding extra deflection over its existing 63.5mm thickness in front and 9.5mm towards the rear. There was also room in the superstructure roof for hatches for the driver and co-driver. Underneath, however, the transmission and power pack (a Continental W-670 petrol engine) were the same, the latter with all its inherent problems. Apart from the fact that it used high octane aircraft fuel, which heavily constrained its range, it also suffered from some peculiar faults, particularly on start up. First the seven-cylinder radial engine needed to be rotated by hand some forty times to redistribute the oil that had pooled in the bottom cylinders. It also had a tendency to backfire on start-up, which could ignite unburnt fuel and start a fire in the engine. There were fire extinguishers in the engine compartment for just such contingencies but these tended to freeze the engine solid for quite some time. For this reason most crews preferred to open the rear doors and stand ready with fire extinguishers. Apart from that it was a robust tank, with none of the mechanical problems that plagued British tanks around the time of the introduction of the first Stuart tanks in 1941. Though it retained the manual transmission, the front-sited transmission and sprockets gave a more positive control for the driver.

The recce version was developed as a result of the conditions the Allies found in Italy. Within a short space of time they had come to the realisation that this was not great country for tank operations, the terrain limiting where they could operate and what they could do. Thus, while there was a need for the medium tanks that the Allies took there, light tanks like the Stuart proved to be less than useful. This led to the development of the recce version of the Stuart III. Removal of the turret opened up the fighting compartment, into which seats for two crewmen were installed, along with extra radio gear in the hull sponsons. This left the crew quite vulnerable, so a hexagonal armoured lip was welded around the hole left by the turret, and a pintle mount and shield for a .50 calibre Browning machine gun installed in front. Additional firepower was provided by retaining the hull machine gun.

Company D, 760 Tank Battalion was also equipped with Stuart tanks, though they had the later model M5A1 Light Tank (Stuart V in British service). These tanks were fitted with twin Cadillac V8 petrol engines, which had twin hydramatic transmissions operating through a transfer case that led to fully automatic gear changes controlled by engine speed alone. The tank, like earlier marks, had controlled differential steering, the steering levers also acting as brakes. Compared to the Sherman tank, it was fast, with a top speed of 58kph. The main armament was a 37mm M6 gun for which there were 147 rounds in the tank. In addition it had three .30 calibre Browning machine guns, one in the hull, one co-axially mounted with the main gun in the turret and the third in a pintle mount on the outside. A total of 6,750 rounds of ammunition was carried for them. Armour ranged from 63mm frontally to 10mm in the rear. It had a crew of four men, the driver and co-driver sitting on either side of the transmission in the hull. For vision they had access to periscopes in their access hatches in the roof. The other two crewmen consisted of the commander/loader in the turret and on his left the gunner. Access to the turret was by way of two hatches in the turret roof.

Company D, 760 Tank Battalion was equipped with seventeen M5A1s and essentially acted as the reconnaissance element of the battalion, the other three companies each having seventeen Shermans, usually a mixture of the radial-engined M4 or M4A1 Medium Tank. In structure, Company D had a Headquarters Platoon of two tanks and three platoons of five tanks each, though each platoon could be further split up in combat into a platoon headquarters tank and two sections of two tanks each. The company was commanded by 1st Lieutenant Herman R. Crowder, while the three platoons were commanded by Second Lieutenant Chester M. Wright, 1 Platoon; Second Lieutenant James W. de Wright, 2 Platoon; and Second Lieutenant John A. Crews, 3 Platoon (see Appendix 2).[2]

In addition, Company D had the support of three 105mm Howitzer Motor Carriage M7s from the Headquarters Company of 760 Tank Battalion, under the command of Lieutenant Victor F. Hipkiss. Known as the Priest in British circles because of its pulpit-like machine gun ring for a .50 calibre Browning, the 105mm HMC M7 was a conversion from the now obsolete M3 Medium Tank. This particular vehicle mounted the US 105mm M1A2, M2 or M2A1 howitzer slightly off-centre in an open-topped compartment of armour ranging from 62mm to 12mm thickness. It had a total crew of seven, consisting of a commander, a driver and a gun crew of five men. Total stowage was 68 rounds of 105mm ammunition and 300 rounds for the .50 calibre machine gun.

The New Zealanders were latecomers to Revenge Force but their Sherman tanks brought much-needed firepower to the assault group. When it was finally equipped with tanks in Egypt, 4 NZ Armoured Brigade was issued with the Sherman III. Like the Stuart tank, the Sherman had a much higher profile than its nearest German counterparts, a consequence of the need to fit a nine-cylinder radial aircraft engine into the first models produced and provide sufficient clearance between the turret basket and the drive shaft. Once again production needs resulted in different engines being fitted in later models and the Sherman III had the GM 6046 diesel engine, essentially conjoined 6-71 diesel engines. Its top speed was 40kph. Like all models of this tank, the Sherman III was equipped with a 75mm gun and a co-axial .30 calibre Browning machine gun in the turret, along with another .30 calibre Browning in the hull. Armour thickness ranged from 89mm to 50mm on the turret and from 64mm to 38mm on the hull. Total ammunition stowage for the 75mm gun was 97 rounds plus 4,750 for the Browning machine guns, most of which was stored in bins in the sponsons or under the turret basket behind the co-driver. The tank crew consisted of five men, two of whom were located in the hull, with the driver to the left of the transmission, steering the tank by way of levers that operated brakes in the differential housing, and the co-driver to the right of the transmission behind the hull machine gun. Access to their positions was via hatches in the hull roof, both of which were fitted with periscopes for vision purposes. In case of emergencies there was also an escape hatch behind the spare driver's seat, while the driver could get access to the fighting compartment of the turret through a gap in the turret basket when the gun was pointing straight ahead. The other three men were located in the turret, with the tank commander under the cupola, which was the sole external access to the turret in the Sherman III model issued to the New Zealanders. In front of the tank commander was the gunner and on the other side of the turret was the loader/radio operator, with the radio itself, the standard British No. 19 set, located in the bustle at the rear of the turret. For vision each man had a periscope, the commander's in the cupola, while the gunner's periscope was connected to the gun by way of a linkage system that kept it and the gun aligned. The gunner also had a telescopic sight. There was a pistol port on the loader's side of the turret. Turret traverse was either by hand crank or by electric hydraulic drive, while the gun could be elevated manually or via hydraulic power. The gun was also fitted with a gyrostabiliser.

Like the other two squadrons of 20 NZ Armoured Regiment, C Squadron was equipped with sixteen Sherman IIIs (see Appendix 2), while there were a further four Sherman IIIs in Regimental Headquarters and eighteen Lynx scout cars in Headquarters Squadron. Each squadron was organised on the basis of a Squadron Headquarters of four tanks and four troops of three tanks each. The regiment also used a system of numbers painted on the hull side to uniquely identify each tank in battle: Squadron HQ tanks were numbers 15–18, while in C Squadron 9 Troop tanks took the numbers 3–5, 10 Troop, 6–8, 11 Troop, 9–11; and 12 Troop, 12–14. In each troop the numbers were allocated in ascending order to the troop officer (either a lieutenant or a second lieutenant), then the troop sergeant and finally the troop corporal. In C Squadron, the squadron commander Major Pat Barton had tank number 15, while his second-in-command (2iC) Captain Pat Abbott had number 16. Generally, 2iC Abbott's responsibilities in the squadron were more administrative, such as maintaining contact with the B Echelon, but in combat he took on the role of rear link, maintaining contact with either Regimental HQ or the unit to which the squadron was attached. Tank number 17 was that of Captain Jim Moodie, the battle captain. Should anything happen to Barton or Barton's tank, Moodie would take over command of the squadron. Alternatively, if the squadron were to be split in two for an operation, Moodie would take command of two of its troops. The last tank in Squadron HQ was that of Sergeant Major Jock Laidlaw.

Chapter 6

The Token Texan Tankers

As a unit, 760 Tank Battalion could trace its origins back to 1941. It was then that Second Lieutenant Richard Langston from 68 Armored Regiment at Fort Benning, Georgia, was ordered to take a cadre of recruits to Camp Bowie in Texas to help form the new unit. As Langston later recalled, it was a place that had its merits and disadvantages:

> Benning was wet and cold that winter with the only heat from Sibley stoves, and outdoor latrines and showers. Officers attended tank driving classes to learn the art of double clutching gears without stripping them. But we learned a great deal under the personal supervision of then Col. George Patton who had the habit of showing up in the field unexpectedly in his Packard convertible.[1]

The journey to Camp Bowie took four days and nights, and was another shock for the cadre. For Second Lieutenant John W. Humes it was:

> Hot-hot-hot – no trees – just mesquite – caliche rock – and huge jack rabbits. Sand – brush – and so hot the newly laid asphalt roads just melted in the 110–115 degree heat.[2]

Once there, they were assigned a site at the furthest corner of the camp, the unit suspecting that 'those in command at the camp did not want to expose the pure-blooded[3] Texan Division to people that had experienced life in thirty-eight different states'. It did, however, give the unit ready access to 'all of the training areas and our tanks did not tear up the camp roads whenever the order came to "move out"'. The initial cadre of thirty-five men was soon built up to a strength of 255 enlisted men, both Regular Army from 2 Armored Division and draftees, all of whom had been posted to the unit on a one-year commitment. On 1 June 1941 Lieutenant Colonel Donald F. Spalding took over command of the battalion.

As first conceived, the unit was a light tank battalion with only four companies (HQ, A, B and C) plus administrative units, but no tanks. Instead they had to train with jeeps, 0.75-ton Dodges, 2.5-ton GMCs,

White half-tracks and scout cars. The first tanks they received were the twin-turreted M2A2 Light Tank, dubbed 'Mae Wests', and later the M2A3 Light Tank with its single turret. Radio control in them was non-existent, and the commander was reduced to using his feet to communicate with the driver. Being under strength also meant that everybody in the unit had to learn everything from operations with tanks to maintenance of equipment. By November, when the battalion had received a total of twelve tanks, it was redesignated as a medium tank battalion, and at the end of the month, amid great excitement, nine M3 Medium tanks arrived. Then, on 7 December, the Japanese attacked Pearl Harbor and the US entered the war. For the battalion personnel it meant that their tour of duty had been extended for the duration.

On 24 June the battalion personnel were notified that they were going to move back to Fort Benning. As some noted, 'New barracks were being built to replace tents, so naturally it was time for a move.'[4] At Benning things were better. They started off being quartered in real barracks, not tents (with no rattlesnakes under the floor), only later to move into one-storey buildings on stilts. Though they were still to undertake their own training, their assigned role was that of the Demonstration Battalion for the Infantry School. This involved putting on demonstrations to show the capability of tanks in support of infantry or how to defend against tanks. Robert F. Moore recalled one of these:

> In one unit of instruction, students dug a pit in the ground called a 'tank trap'. We drove a tank into it, made a feeble attempt to get out and then stopped. After the students left we had to get the tank out, which sometimes took some digging but could usually be accomplished by simply driving the tank out. One day I was in too much of a hurry and had to pull the tank out before all the students had departed the area. A whole squad of infantry school instructors descended on me and chewed me out for destroying the confidence of the students.[5]

From Benning the battalion moved to Camp Prickett in Virginia, training with 3 Armored Division, with the equipment they were expected to use in combat. It was there they received their overseas movement orders. At midday on 13 January they entrained for Staten Island, New York, transferring to the USAT *Jon Ericson* on arrival and setting sail for Morocco the next day. After reaching Casablanca on 24 January they spent a month at a camp opposite the cemetery outside the city before moving to a cork forest outside Rabat. Here they were brought up to strength for the Tunisian campaign, Companies A, B and C receiving M4 and M4A1 Medium Tanks, which they painted in desert trim. On 26 April they were sent to Port Lyautey to guard the border with Spanish Morocco, a move that was made with 191 and 757 Tank Battalions. A month later, the war in Tunisia over, 760 Tank Battalion found itself in the unenviable position of being prepared to fight but apparently with nowhere to go. Nevertheless, with plans afoot to invade Sicily, and ultimately Italy, Company A was sent by rail to Magenta in Algeria on 10 June in preparation for the invasion, the rest of the battalion following in September.

In October the entire battalion sailed for Italy, landing at Bagnoli. Here they were reorganised once again, a reconnaissance company (Company D) being added and equipped with the M5A1 Light Tank. There they remained until 1 December on garrison duty, reverting to the US Fifth Army command when it moved to Dugenta, north of the Volturno river. It was hardly an inspiring introduction to Italy, as Company B's commander, Captain John E. Krebs, recalled later:

> Dugenta was a 'mud hole'. Tanks and wheeled vehicles that moved around in the bivouac area would get stuck in the mud, and it was freezing cold to boot. We walked in the mud, ate in the mud, and slept in the mud. Although we had tents for sleeping, I recalled the makeshift stoves that we attempted to use to keep ourselves warm in the tents.[6]

Late in December 1943 Company B was called upon to provide fire support for US and Canadian special forces in their assault on Monte Maio but this was to be short-lived. Cold freezing rain started to fall in torrents, bringing the American assault to a halt. In January 1944 the Fifth Army renewed its attack on the remaining defensive bastions before Cassino, all three companies of the battalion providing fire support for the infantry attack on Monte Porchia and San Vittore. On 8 January the battalion was attached to 34 Division, supporting attacks on Monte Chaia and Cervaro, before taking part in the softening up of Monte Trocchio. Fortunately the Germans abandoned the latter before the final attack was launched, perhaps realising that their position there had become untenable.

With Monte Trocchio secured, the next move was on the Liri valley itself. Thus, when 36 Division was assigned the job of forcing a crossing over the Gari river in the vicinity of Sant'Angelo in Theodice, 760 Tank Battalion was ordered to provide support. On 20 January Company B moved into an assembly area south of Sant'Angelo, there to provide direct support for 143 Infantry Regiment. Unfortunately, it proved impossible to get the tanks any closer than 500–700 yards from the river, so instead they found some good firing positions on ridges overlooking the area. As it so happened, the infantry attack that night failed and the troops who did cross the Gari were soon forced to withdraw. More success was had the following night. Two infantry regiments managed to gain a limited bridgehead by the morning of 22 January but the failure to launch tank-capable bridges over the Gari ultimately doomed the whole operation. Throughout this period Company B remained in position and fired on what targets the infantry could point out, each tank platoon taking turns to move up and down the front to fire on enemy positions on the opposite bank. On 24 January a truce was arranged at 11.15am to allow medical teams on both sides to retrieve their wounded and dead. As Krebs later noted:

> At 1106 hours, 'B' Company ceased fire. It was quiet and no gunshots were heard. Most of the tank men dismounted and were behind their tanks along with some of the infantrymen as it was now time for the truce to begin. I then observed the river and beyond the west bank and was alerted to a battery of four or five Nebelwerfers that were firing towards our tanks. We were over five minutes into the truce. Two infantrymen about 25 yards away were hit by a shell. Sgt George Lenkalis left his protected area to rescue the soldiers and was mortally wounded by an incoming shell. Another infantry soldier was also wounded. Sgt Vernon Marshall, Sgt Raymond Taylor and I immediately ran out to help in the rescue, and we were able to get the three soldiers behind the command tank. We managed to apply first aid to one of the infantrymen and, as we began to examine Sgt Lenkalis's wounds, he died within seconds. By now we were 15 minutes into the truce and medical personnel and litter bearers were out on the field picking up the wounded and the dead.[7]

With the failure of the Texans' attack, 760 Tank Battalion adopted a defensive role, Company B moving north around Monte Trocchio and taking up firing positions near the banks of the Gari river along the bed of the old railway, which led up to the destroyed bridge. On the afternoon of 1 February four anti-tank guns sited near the railway station came in for some attention from the company, the tanks receiving fire from 150mm artillery in return. On 3 February they became engaged in a duel with some German tanks near the railway station:

> After we fired more than 100 rounds, the enemy tanks withdrew. Three enemy tanks were left on the battlefield. After we adjusted our artillery and tank fire on the Nebelwerfers, they were silenced.[8]

Prior to the launch of the Second Battle of Cassino on 15 February, Company B was withdrawn several hundred yards for safety, so as to be out of range of the bombing of the monastery. Five days later it was moved to a holding area on the southwestern edge of Monte Trocchio on a two-hour alert for exploitation up the Liri valley, a move that never happened with the collapse of the second offensive. Then, on 22 February, orders were received for Company B to line up on the southeastern slopes of Monte Trocchio in preparation for an attack on the railway station. The attack did not happen and all they received for their trouble was an attack by German Stukas, some of the tanks suffering damage from the dive-bombing and strafing. As Krebs later related:

> All tanks quickly mounted their 50 caliber machine guns. The aircraft returned and we gave them a hot reception. With seventeen tanks firing tracer [and] armour-piercing bullets we achieved success. Lt Cox's 2nd Platoon was credited with destroying one Stuka and damaging another – as it was left smoking as though on fire. I personally fired the command tank 50 caliber, and it was good to see the tracers slamming into the enemy aircraft as they flew away in smoke.[9]

Another 24 hours later the company received a hand-carried message: 'British Eighth Army taking over this sector of the front from the Fifth US Army, New Zealand Tank Group to attack the RR Station.'

Chapter 7

Tank Killers Turned Tank Men

Like the rest of the tank force that went up Cavendish Road, C Squadron, 20 NZ Armoured Regiment, was a mixture of men of different experiences. The squadron, in fact, was made up of those who had fought as infantry in the North African campaign and others who had trained on tanks in New Zealand before joining the reformed armoured unit in Egypt. Thus Major Pat Barton, Captain Jim Moodie, Captain Pat Abbott and Sergeant Theo Dore were 'old digs', who had seen service in the desert war. In contrast, Lieutenant Jack Hazlett, better known as 'Stuffy', had come direct from New Zealand.

At the time of the return of 2 New Zealand Division to Egypt in June 1942 to help stem the advance of Rommel's Afrika Korps, Moodie was a lieutenant in command of a portée-mounted 2-pounder anti-tank gun in 20 NZ Battalion. While the British struggled to form a defensive line at El Alamein, 2 NZ division was ordered to take up a position at Minqar Qaim to the south of Mersa Matruh with the object of denying the escarpment to the advancing German forces. Lieutenant Jim Moodie vividly recalled the occasion many years later:

> About 8 o'clock in the morning the sun was rising and you could see the vehicles. In the heat of the day the mirage effect became worse, much greater as the sun came up. A vehicle, an ordinary truck, looked four times higher in the mirage. You could spot the enemy miles away and they would gradually come closer. It might take three to four hours. I was on anti-tank 2-pounders. I wasn't dug in. I had to change positions smartly; move back out of one position and come up into a new position. You had to keep silent, under 400 yards was okay, even under that depending on what you were aiming for. The idea was to wait, play doggo until they got closer and you could get a shot off. I mean the whole place was a mass of advancing enemy and you didn't know who was shooting at who. It was a mad house. While we were knocking off his transports or tanks, somebody from the

Lieutenant Jim Moodie's anti-tank crew with their 2-pounder portée after their return to Egypt in June 1942. (*Jim Moodie*)

opposition was concentrating on you, though you were quite unaware of this.[1]

First blood fell to men in the battalion's 9 Platoon, who allowed some Germans driving a captured porteé 2-pounder to close up to their position before opening fire and killing most of its crew. On the afternoon of 27 June, as the advancing German column split and began encircling the New Zealanders, Moodie took over the No. 1 position on one of the 2-pounders and successfully destroyed two troop carriers, then:

> I happened to be No. 1 on the gun, Ken Skinner was the loader and a Jerry armour-piercing [round] came through the shield and hit the breechblock. It was diverted into me and it put a chunk of metal into my thigh.[2]

Ordering the crew to the safety of their slit trench, Moodie personally retrieved their portée, then collected his crew and drove back up the

Sergeant Theo Dore. (*Michael Dore*)

escarpment; once their gun was repaired, they returned to the front line. Later Moodie and Sergeant McConchie drove out to the captured portée and towed it back to their lines. For this action Moodie was awarded the Military Cross.[3]

Sergeant Theo Dore was also with the battalion at Minqar Qaim and took part in the spectacular breakout of the division to get back to the British lines at El Alamein:

> A shot was fired and then we started to go faster, break into a run, rifles at the ready, Bren gunners and away we go. It was all go. It was such a hell of a surprise for the Germans that some of them were still in their sleep, coming out to see what was going on. They wouldn't get any further from the side of the truck. Awful business. Tracers and bombs, drove right through. Attempted to form us up but that didn't work, the trucks came through. Wonderful arrangement. Broke ranks because we knew what to do, what was happening. The trucks were there to pick us up. No order given and you jumped on the nearest truck you could get onto.[4]

With a loose defensive line established at El Alamein, the battle for control of Egypt developed around a series of strategic points, Ruweisat Ridge among them. Though no more than 150–200m higher than the ground around it, it was hardly a ridge in the classical sense but whoever controlled it could dominate the area around it with observed artillery fire. On the night of 14 July 4 NZ Brigade launched an attack on Ruweisat Ridge. At this time Pat Barton, then a captain, was in command of 20 NZ Battalion's anti-tank platoon of three 2-pounders:

> We arrived over the ridge under a hail of fire and AP shells, not knowing if it was Ruweisat or not. It was a hull-down position, which was all we craved at the moment. The guns were put into the only position which offered any protection [the north side of the ridge] and then the task was to find the 20 Bn.[5]

In fact Barton discovered that they were well to the north of the battalion, though not totally alone as behind them were some 6-pounder anti-tank guns from 7 NZ Anti-tank Regiment. At dawn the following morning they came under fire from six or seven German tanks to the west, forcing them to pull back over the ridge. Here Barton sited their portée but it was soon knocked out by an armour-piercing round that wrecked the engine. Things then quietened down until later that afternoon when one of his 2-pounder porteés was ordered to accompany two 6-pounder portées, both of which were hit, one of them catching fire. By this stage 20 NZ Battalion had been largely overrun and, on seeing the portées withdrawing, Barton made his way back along the southern side of Ruweisat Ridge until:

> To my utter amazement and joy I beheld a squadron of Grant tanks on the flat ground to the southeast. They moved forward to within 400 yards of the Ridge and then stopped. They fired a few rounds and then one troop came right up to the Ridge and fired a few rounds over the top. By then I really thought we were going to get everything back. I ran over to one of the tanks and climbed on board. The commander appeared – an NCO. I told him my story and asked if they were going in and he said he didn't know. I tried to impress on him the urgency and to get on to his commander – I probably wasn't very tactful I'm afraid – but just then he whipped his headphones on and said they had orders to retire and move somewhere else – and they did! I don't know quite what I did – I was speechless with rage, impotent and disappointed.[6]

Barton luckily escaped the debacle at Ruweisat Ridge; he and the other survivors of the battalion, along with the rest of 4 NZ Brigade, were eventually pulled out of the line and sent back to Maadi Camp to rest and refit.

Dore also made it back to their own lines, having had to walk out when the German armour finally came in:

> We had a fellow from Dunedin called Williams [...] we were laying down behind some rocks and I stopped a bit of shrapnel there, just missed my hamstring, and I could hardly walk. So [me] and another one of our guys were wounded and this chap Williams he said 'I'll go over here and see if I can get one of these trucks for these wounded fellows away.' It was one of our trucks alright but one the Germans had confiscated. He went over and as soon as they saw him they just said thank you very much, another prisoner. So we had to walk out and struggle out. We had none of our compasses, we didn't have an officer with us. But we knew where we had to go and just when the North Star came into view and we went on through the night.[7]

After a spell in hospital Dore was posted not to his own unit but to 26 NZ Battalion, taking part in the Second Battle of Alamein. On the night of

23 October, around 11.15pm, he crossed the start line with the rest of the battalion:

> There were German tanks on fire. We were told not in any case to stop for any of our blokes who were wounded because there would have been stretcher bearers coming right behind us. I suppose we must have got to the line where we were expected to go, the target. I had a water bottle on my right hip and it was one of the ones that was covered in canvas and the thing started to flare up a bit and I stopped a bullet that went through the water bottle and into my right hip. It would have probably broken my right leg if it hadn't been for the waterbottle. So I had to be taken out.[8]

When Dore finally returned from hospital he was posted back to his original unit, which, along with the rest of 4 NZ Brigade, was in the process of being converted to armour. This was the result of General Bernard Freyberg's long-held desire to have his own armour within the division, a desire that went back to 1940 but had been thwarted by the British high command in the Middle East. Instead, Freyberg and the New Zealand government had been persuaded to raise a tank brigade in New Zealand for eventual deployment in Egypt. This had all gone well at the start. The personnel for it had been pulled together towards the end of 1941 and the first of the promised thirty Valentine tanks had arrived – and then the Japanese bombed the US naval base at Pearl Harbor in Hawaii. With Japan entering the war on the Axis side, and their subsequent rapid thrust through South East Asia, the New Zealand government was unwilling to release the embryonic 1 NZ Army Tank Brigade to Freyberg anytime soon. However, the inadequate support provided by British armour at Ruweisat Ridge, a situation repeated a week later at the El Mreir Depression, when 6 NZ Brigade was overwhelmed by German armour, resulted in a reversal of the government's decision regarding the tank brigade. Now it agreed to the release of the 3rd Battalion (3 Tanks) from the brigade at the end of 1942 to reinforce the depleted units of 4 NZ Armoured Brigade (as it had become known). More were to follow the next year.[9]

As a result of this decision, 20 NZ Armoured Regiment saw an influx of new personnel, among them 'Stuffy' Hazlett from Southland. At the beginning of the war Hazlett had been posted to this unit from 5 Otago Hussars, one of nine mounted rifle regiments, where he had held the rank of lieutenant since 1940. At that time the Hussars still had their horses and continued to train with them into 1941. In March 1941 they had taken part

Lieutenant Jack 'Stuffy' Hazlett (left) leads a column from 5 Otago Mounted Rifles through Peel Forest during manoeuvres of 3 Mounted Rifle Brigade in 1941. (*Katherine Hazlett*)

in a three-month training camp in Canterbury with their sister regiments 1 Canterbury Yeomanry Cavalry and 10 Nelson Marlborough Mounted Rifles. At the culmination of this camp the mounted regiments took part in an extensive set of manoeuvres in South Canterbury, but it would be the last time they operated with horses. By the end of that year the New Zealand Army had switched to mechanised transport, albeit at the start using a lot of impressed civilian vehicles. So the mounted regiments lost their horses. Before this happened, however, Hazlett was posted to the embryonic tank brigade but not to the South Island battalion, 3 Tanks. Instead he found himself in the Brigade Headquarters Squadron. As a result he remained in New Zealand when the brigade was broken up at the end of October 1942. His unit was sent down to the South Island and based outside Christchurch. Seven months later, in 1943, it too was broken up and its personnel dispatched to Egypt to build 4 NZ Armoured Brigade up to full strength.

The New Zealand Division was eventually shipped over to Italy in October 1943, joining the Eighth Army on the Adriatic coast. In November the division launched an assault over the Sangro river that ultimately brought it up to the Castel Frentano Ridge, where it came face to face with its nemesis: the town of Orsogna on the next ridge. Three attempts were made to capture Orsogna but it was not until the third attack that 20 NZ Armoured Regiment became involved. The initial assault up the Sfasciata Ridge was made by 18 NZ Armoured Regiment and 5 NZ Brigade on 15 December. However, by the time they cut the road to Ortona the losses they had suffered had left them too weak to exploit towards Orsogna. Accordingly C Squadron of 20 NZ Armoured Regiment under Major Pat Barton was ordered up the ridge. Barton's orders indicated that once there, they were to pass through the advanced positions towards Orsogna, possibly with some support from two companies from 28 Maori Battalion. The trouble was, no one had told the Maori Battalion and by the time its units were ordered to join Barton's tanks it would have been too late in the day to attack so C Squadron was ordered to go in alone. What happened next was a charge in true cavalry fashion as the squadron burst out from behind the Orsogna cemetery and drove at speed down the road. Within minutes, three tanks were hit and caught fire, followed by several more shortly afterwards. Theo Dore, in the leading troop, had vivid memories of what happened to him:

> We went tanks in line over the railway line and across the meadows and struck these haystacks, looked like the old fashioned wheat stooks but there were also some other small stacks, some of which contained German infantry and some of them were small machine guns. Of course we relished that and of course they had no show. We cleaned up a lot of that stuff and we were heading for a spot in Orsogna on the outskirts of the city itself and a big haystack in our wake straight ahead. It wasn't a haystack at all, it was a German Mk IV tank with its gun pointed straight at us waiting, waiting for us, come on boys. So he cleaned us up with three armour piercing shells through the turret and five through the hull. The driver was killed, the wireless operator was killed and the gunner was killed, McGavin the lap gunner, the spare driver, got out through the hatch at the bottom. When I came to, the wireless operator was on the floor, had a look at him 'Oh crikey not much I can do there'; I wouldn't have been able to lift a body and get him out through there because he was dead. It was on fire, there was shrapnel and stuff going around and flames coming from somewhere, might have been down in the front motor. 'I have to get out of this, Dore'. Well I had my black beret on

Sergeant Theo Dore's Sherman tank penetrated further into German lines than the others in C Squadron after being hit several times. The reason: the driver was dead with his foot still depressing the accelerator pedal. (*Gerhard Pohle*)

and earphones and I went to throw myself over the top and came to the length of the cord and came back again. When I got back I threw this stuff off. I was burnt pretty badly and shrapnel on my arms. I remember hitting the ground and the old tank was going about two miles an hour, it was still moving.[10]

Dore's tank continued to move towards Orsogna until his officer, Lieutenant Percy Brooks, climbed onto it and stopped it; Dore's driver was dead with his foot hard on the accelerator pedal. The attack eventually had to be called off and the remnants of the squadron returned to the cemetery.

C Squadron accompanied A Squadron and the Maori Battalion in another attack the next day but the German paratroopers who had been brought in to defend Orsogna were ready for them. Within a short while they had forced the Maori infantry to ground and turned their attention to the tanks, picking them off one by one. The outcome was the same; the attack failed and the survivors were forced to pull back to the cemetery.

For Pat Barton it was a highly unsatisfactory situation and not what they had trained to do or expected to happen. Many good men had been killed and others lost through injury, among them his battle captain, Alan Shand, who nearly died while walking out of their RAP when a piece of shrapnel severed a major artery in his leg. After the battle Pat Barton replaced Shand with Jim Moodie, by this stage a captain.

Both Ruweisat Ridge and El Mreir Depression had taught the New Zealanders that infantry could not do without tank support. The division had formed its own armoured unit so that this situation would not arise again. Now they had learned that tanks could not do without infantry. All they could hope for now was that it would not happen again.

PART II

THE EXECUTION OF REVENGE

Chapter 8

Bradman Begins

Lieutenant General Bernard Freyberg had initially hoped that Operation Dickens could be launched around 28 February but heavy rain, typical for the time of year, set in. This did not stop Lieutenant General Mark Clark from urging him to stop waiting for ideal weather and go ahead with the attack, saying: 'I fully realise that we are not going to completely break through and the tanks will only play a small part in the attack.'[1] Freyberg, however, could not be moved on this. Part of his problem was the variation in the weather over the whole of Italy. When it was clear at Cassino, it might be difficult to launch aircraft from the Allied airfields at Naples, Foggia, Corsica, Sardinia and further back in North Africa. There was also the requirement imposed on him by Alexander of three preliminary fine days before the attack.[2] The weather did start to clear early in March but even after the rain had stopped there was the need to wait at least another week for the ground to dry out both around Cassino and at Foggia where the planes would fly from.

Dickens was eventually set for 15 March. On the appointed day the medium bombers appeared promptly at 8.30am and started to unleash their hate on the town, the codename for this operation being Bradman. Within minutes Cassino was engulfed in flames and dust as the detonations of the bombs rent the air. The medium bombers were followed by the heavy B-17 Flying Fortresses, which continued the assault, ceasing bombing at midday. By the end of it, terrible destruction had been wrought, not only on Cassino and its defenders, but on the area around the town. At least 80 per cent of the bombs from the medium bombers had fallen in the town, but only half of those dropped by their heavier cousins had done so. The rest had come down on the slopes of Monte Cassino or in the Rapido valley, while some had even struck a French hospital further up the Rapido valley at Venafro.

Unfortunately for the Allies, the hoped-for demoralising effect of the bombing and of the subsequent artillery barrage on Cassino's German defenders was somewhat limited. The town had been reduced to ruins

The attack on Cassino township was preceded by a massive aerial bombardment, seen here from the other side of the Rapido valley. In this view the castle on Rocco Ianula has just emerged from the smoke and dust. (*Alexander Turnbull Library*)

and no more than one or two buildings survived intact. Although many paratroopers disappeared in the bombing, never to be seen again, enough managed to struggle out of their cellars and caves to face the attackers as they came in. As a portent of things to come, a sizeable body of Germans managed to survive the bombing by taking shelter in a cave behind the Hotel Excelsior-Continental. They were joined shortly after the cessation of the bombing by a party of pioneers. In addition, one of their supporting assault guns and its crew in the building next door escaped unharmed, as did a tank and its crew further down the road. Reinforced by more men and anti-tank guns that night, they were able to turn this area into a formidable strongpoint.

With the bombing over, it was the turn of the artillery, aided by fighter-bombers, to further soften up the town as the assaulting infantry from 25 NZ Battalion began their attack. While the battalion had no trouble regaining their old positions around the gaol, they started to run into trouble when they tried to push further into the town. Far from being the pushover the New Zealanders had been led to expect, the paratroopers were putting up serious resistance and the attacking companies soon broke up into smaller groups as they struggled forward. To add to their problems, radio communications with Battalion Headquarters started to break down.

The situation was no better for the men of 19 NZ Armoured Regiment. It proved impossible to push tanks into the town along two of the pre-designated routes, so some tanks were forced to retrace their steps and use the road running along the base of the Cassino massif. Moreover, the worst fears of the air force liaison officers had been realised – the bombing had wrecked the town to the extent that the crews were forced to get out of their tanks and make a passage for them using picks and shovels. Fortunately it was not all bad news; one troop was able to get into a position from where its guns could engage targets on Castle Hill.

For 25 NZ Battalion progress through the town was slow. By 2.00pm they should have been on Phaseline Quisling, but B Company had only got as far as a building known as the Nunnery (Chiesa and Monastica di San Scholastica) in the northern part of the town and by mid-afternoon had gained the shelter of a school but could make no further progress thanks to small-arms fire from Castle Hill. In the meantime A Company on the left made more headway. By 3.30pm they had fought their way further south to the northern branch of Route 6. Here, with the support of some tanks that had managed to close up to the post office, one platoon crossed the road and entered a building that became known as the Convent (Chiesa del Carmine). Unfortunately, the Germans already held part of the building and could not be dislodged so the platoon was forced to retreat. Another platoon reached the post office but was unable to advance any further westwards.

The one real success of the day occurred on the right flank, where D Company of the battalion had gone ahead without their promised tank support and launched an assault on Castle Hill. Here the company split into two platoons, one moving round to the eastern ridge, while the other worked their way up the perilously steep northern face. This worked in a most spectacular fashion, this platoon surprising the headquarters of the castle defenders in their bunker and taking them prisoner. Then, while the troops in the castle were distracted by this attack, they were caught by the sudden arrival of the other platoon behind them and were soon forced to surrender.

Castle Hill, seen here from above Point 165, was the scene of intense fighting on 19 March that ultimately spelt the end of the Gurkha/Essex attack on the monastery. (*Tom Sherlock*)

The capture of the castle was the cue for 4 Indian Division troops to move up and occupy it in preparation for their phase of the assault. Unfortunately, the attack was now seriously behind schedule, with only one of the objective lines having been reached by the New Zealand troops and then only partially. Worse still, thanks to the uncoupling of the two arms of the attack, the Indians appeared to go about their next stage of the operation in complete ignorance of this. This was an eventuality that Freyberg had hoped to avoid in his original plan.

The job of 5 Indian Brigade was to capture the monastery and they set about achieving this once 1/4 Essex Regiment had taken over from 25 NZ Battalion at the castle and occupied Point 165 beyond it. Not that the brigade was very successful: 1/6 Rajputana Rifles failed completely in their attempts to secure the two bends in the serpentine road they had been assigned and by morning were back at the castle. However, that night a company of 1/9 Gurkha Rifles managed to slip through the German Forward Defence Localities and reach Hangman's Hill. It was another spectacular achievement but, unfortunately, one that was to impose a constraint on the future activities of the Indians as their efforts became focused on first securing a corridor up to the Gurkhas and later just keeping them resupplied. Nightfall also brought with it torrential rain that filled up craters and cellars and generally made life miserable for the troops in the town. It also brought with it reinforcements in the form of 26 NZ Battalion, and one company of 24 NZ Battalion.

Chapter 9

Into the Mire

It was not until 16 March that the Indians had become aware of the success of the Gurkhas. Sometime later that morning they saw some figures moving around on Hangman's Hill but it was only when they were about to bombard the position that they picked up a weak radio signal and realised that it was the missing company of Gurkhas. Meanwhile in Cassino the New Zealand troops had made some inroads into the town after engineers bridged the Rapido along Route 6. This achieved, a tank from 19 NZ Armoured Regiment managed to make its way along Route 6 and, under its supporting fire, 26 NZ Battalion moved in and took the Convent. Elsewhere troops from 24 and 25 NZ Battalions, in an attempt to clear out the town under Castle Hill, came under heavy fire and were forced to give up what little ground they had taken. Their supporting tanks from 19 Armoured Regiment made little progress and when one squadron was pulled back later that evening they found that only three of them could move; the other seven were mired or damaged and had to be left behind.

That evening at 6.00pm Freyberg rang Galloway to suggest that they reinforce the Gurkhas on Hangman's Hill and prepare to launch an assault on the monastery itself. Galloway's response was that he preferred not to divert 5 Indian Brigade from its original plan but would give consideration to strengthening the hold on Hangman's Hill if circumstances permitted. An hour and a half or so later he called Freyberg to suggest that the best way to clear Cassino town was to send in more infantry, and commented that this was a prerequisite for his force launching an attack on the monastery.[1] Then, at 10.10pm, Clark intervened by getting Major General Alfred M. Gruenther, his chief of staff, to call Freyberg to express his disappointment that no attack was to be launched in the direction from Point 593 and raised the question as to why the tanks could not be sent in from behind Snakeshead Ridge. Freyberg responded by pointing out the difficulties facing Galloway and the necessity of clearing the town first.[2]

The remains of the stanchion for the cable car on Point 435 had the appearance, to those in the Rapido valley, of a hangman's frame, hence the name given to this position on Monte Cassino. The Gurkhas held this position for several days from the start of the Third Battle of Cassino. (*Polish Institute and Sikorski Museum*)

Nevertheless Galloway did relent somewhat on his decision not to reinforce the Gurkhas and that night the rest of their battalion made their way up to join their fellows on Hangman's Hill. On the morning of 17 March Freyberg responded with this message to the commander of 2 NZ Division, Major-General 'Ike' Parkinson, at 8.20am:

> You have to work with great energy to get down to the station. Get them into the sunken road and then work south. That is a first charge and should be got on with straight away. I don't want to bring in a brigade of 78 Div. Com[man]d NZ Div said it was quite unnecessary. Put great energy into cleaning it up on a broad front. It is essential that we should get through to the Grs [Gurkhas on Hangman's Hill] tonight. We have ... [to] establish a route to the people on the hill for maintenance. Anywhere you can push in tanks do so ...[3]

(**Opposite**) Cassino township as it appeared before the war: (**1**) Jail; (**2**) Chiesa di Santa Scholastica (The Nunnery); (**3**) Rocca Ianula (Castle Hill); (**4**) Post Office; (**5**) Municipio (Municipal Buildings); (**6**) Piazza Principe Amedeo (Botanical Gardens); (**7**) Chiesa di San Antonio; (**8**) Chiesa del Carmine (The Convent); (**9**) Hotel Excelsior (Continental); (**10**) Hotel des Roses; (**11**) Funivia (cable-car); (**12**) Railway Station; (**13**) Railway Engine Shed (The Round House); (**14**) to The Baron's Palace.

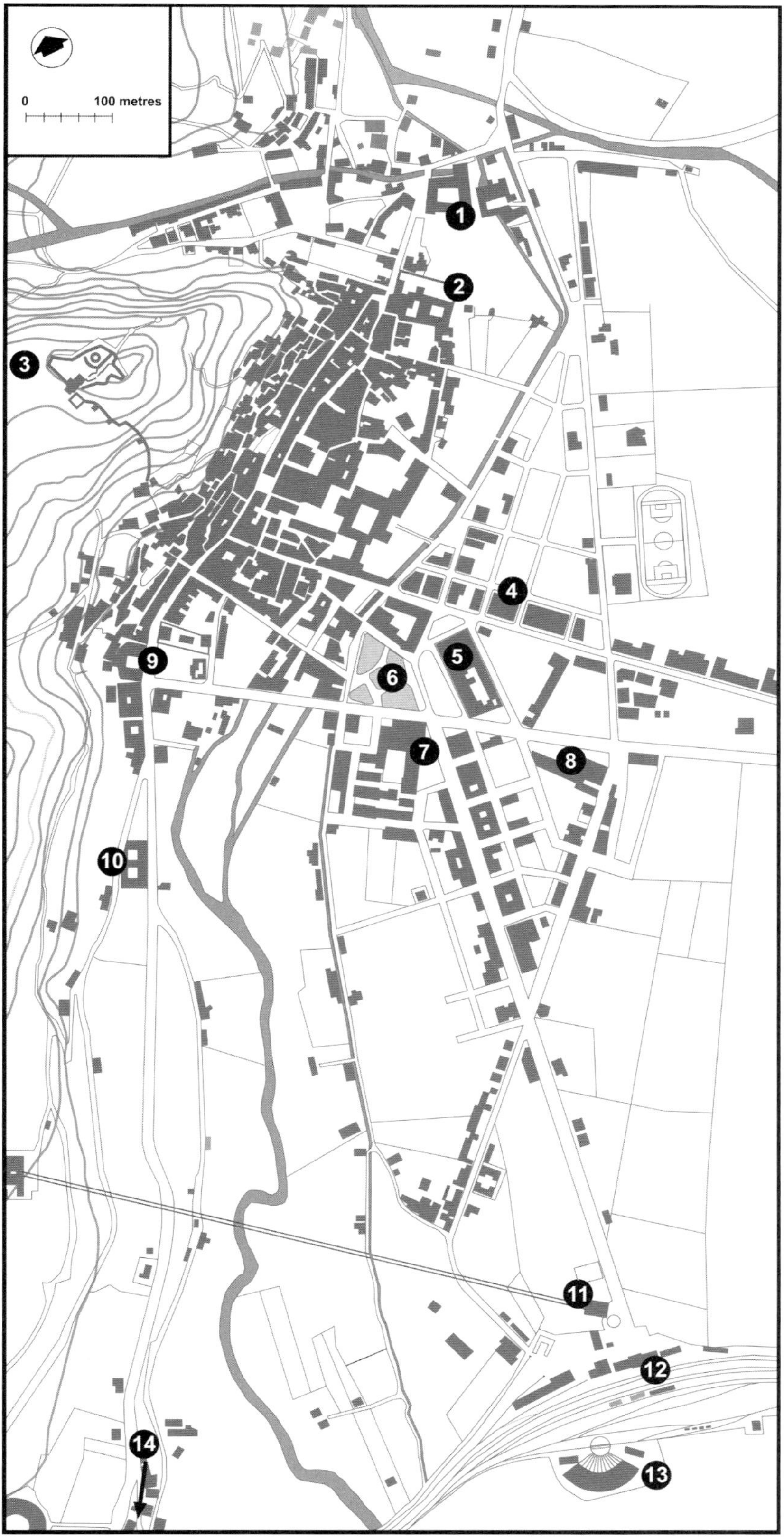

0
100 metres
1
2
3
4
5
6
7
8
9
10
11
12
13
14

Clark rang Freyberg 25 minutes later to again press his concerns over the lack of troops in the town, as Freyberg later noted in his diary:

> Army Comd [Clark] said: 'You keep telling me you have plenty of infantry. I cannot see why the 78 Div cannot start.' GOC [Freyberg] says Parkinson says there is a battalion of infantry doing nothing – no necessity for it. 26 Bn are waiting to go in. Only very small area and we have lots of troops in there already. GOC says we have more tanks than we can use ... we have 350 waiting behind. At present it would not be a bit of use putting them in. Army Comd asked about the Hook [Operation Revenge]. GOC said it will not turn the scale. It is like the Anzio landing. It will only be some good when the front has gone, or when the thing looks like it is going to bits. . . . Army Comd said that GOC had indicated that the hook would be going in and he wondered what had made him change his mind. GOC said that the hook would go in when the Convent was taken and that has not happened . . .[4]

With these talks concluded, Freyberg went forward to the NZ Tactical Headquarters to watch the battle unfold.

The day of 17 March turned out to be one of mixed fortunes. Though the Indians had managed to take Point 236 on the serpentine road above Castle Hill in the night, they lost it just before dawn to a German counter-attack. Thus the Germans had managed to break the corridor between the Gurkhas on Hangman's Hill and the troops below, at the same time as being able to dominate Point 165 and Castle Hill, putting the Essex troops holding the former in a most precarious position. In the town 25 NZ Battalion had been detailed to clean out the area in the southwest corner of Cassino. They had the support of some tanks but some of these soon became bogged down in and around the Botanical Gardens. Nevertheless, the tanks were still able to provide fire support for the infantry, who made good progress until they reached the Gari river, where they became pinned down by heavy fire from around the Hotel Continental.

Things went a little better elsewhere in Cassino. While 26 NZ Battalion was struggling to cross Route 6 under shellfire, some tanks from 19 NZ Armoured Regiment struck off to the south around 1100 hours and by midday had reached the railway station. The infantry took a little longer to join them but by 3.00pm had driven out the Germans and were firmly ensconced, both there and on the Hummocks. However, by now the battalion was too tired and too depleted to secure the western end of Jockey.

With this part of the objective secure, 24 NZ Battalion was ordered forward to capture the area from the Hotel Continental to the Coliseum. However, while trying to penetrate the triangle of land bounded by the Gari, the lower slopes of the massif and Route 6, the battalion soon ran into intense fire. One company was forced back to the northern entrance to the town, while the others sidestepped the area and found themselves alongside the other battalions around the Convent. Thus by nightfall the division was still far from securing its two objectives, their control of Phaseline Quisling extended only to the Gari and, though they had taken the station area, they had not secured a bridgehead over the river itself.

Nevertheless by 1.35pm Freyberg felt sufficiently pleased with progress to ring Clark, recording in his diary:

> [Clark] ... asked whether any decision had been made about the attack from the north with the tanks and the Indians. He said 'I cannot help the feeling that is the thing to do.' ... Army Comd was frightened that reinforcements would come into the station and into the monastery and move fast. GOC said we would attack when Indians had their administration fixed.
>
> Army Comd asked about 78 Div. GOC: 'I do not think there is any room for [more] infantry. Army Comd thought it would be before 78 Div got across the river. GOC said 'But more infantry would increase casualties and achieve no more.' Re attack from the north GOC said we had 1,200 casualties on last occasion. Army Comd replied that was when Cassino and Hangman's Hill were in possession of the enemy. He would like to see a stimulated attack. GOC said it cannot be done owing to the timing ... Army Comd asked whether he assumed attack from Hangman's Hill would be tonight and the other [hook attack] in the morning. GOC said it depended on the administration ... Army Comd's final comment was 'Well I hope she goes.'[5]

At 3.15pm Freyberg rang Galloway at 4 Indian Division Headquarters and noted in his diary afterwards:

> [Galloway] considered that more infantry were needed to clear up the town. GOC explained that neither Gen Parkinson nor Bonifant desired it. Galloway said that he was not taking the monastery until the feeding position is right but that he was sure it would be done tonight if administration [ammunition, food, etc.] was in order. GOC

suggested taking the hill and arranging maintenance by dropping from air. GOC then left for TAC to talk matter over.[6]

Despite these achievements, the whole operation could hardly be considered a success. If anything it had already started to fall behind schedule. As a result Freyberg found himself coming under pressure from both Clark and Galloway to commit more infantry to the assault on the town. That morning Freyberg had considered releasing part of 5 NZ Brigade to occupy the station area and bringing in a brigade from 78 Division. This he was reluctant to do because of his hope to utilise 5 NZ Brigade in the pursuit phase after they had broken through the town. To have sent 5 NZ Brigade in at this stage would have meant this part of his plan had failed. In this he had the support of Parkinson. Clark and Galloway, however, were not happy.[7] As Clark later wrote in his diary:

> The battle of Cassino is progressing slowly. Freyberg's enthusiastic plans are not keeping up to his time schedule ... I have repeatedly told Freyberg from his inception of this plan that aerial bombardment alone has and will never drive a determined enemy from his position. Cassino has again proven this theory, for, although no doubt heavy casualties were inflicted upon the enemy in Cassino, sufficient have remained to hold up our advance and cause severe fighting in the town for the past two days ...

Yet despite this, Clark also wrote: 'Due to General Alexander's direct dealing with Freyberg and the fact that this is an all-British show, I am reluctant to give a direct order to Freyberg.'[8]

The trouble was, Clark had been pressing Freyberg strongly and repeatedly to launch the so-called double envelopment of the monastery from Hangman's Hill and simultaneously, or soon after, the tank attack from Cavendish Road. Freyberg was of the opinion that the armoured thrust would achieve little until the monastery had been secured and that it would only succeed when the German front line had begun to crumble. This depended on the attack on the monastery succeeding and this in turn depended on evicting the Germans from Cassino first. However, Galloway was insisting that his attack on the monastery could not be launched until he had a secure supply route up to Hangman's Hill and that this depended on the complete clearance of the town.

The following morning Galloway again suggested that the problems the New Zealanders were experiencing in the town were due to a shortage of

The Round House at Cassino station and the Hummocks.

infantry. Freyberg was in a more receptive mood and by 7.30am, having considered sending in another battalion, he was all but prepared to commit the whole of 5 NZ Brigade. But an hour later Parkinson told him again that he had enough troops in the town. Freyberg deferred his decision but told Parkinson: 'You must remember that the whole operation is being paralysed until Cassino is cleared up.'

Very little progress was made the following day. The Indians on the hillside had little choice but to hold on to what positions they had. Around dawn 26 NZ Battalion at the railway station fended off a major counter-attack by sixty-two men from Fallschirm-MG-Bataillon I; although the attackers managed to enter the Round House, they were easily driven off, only nineteen of them making it back to their own lines. Elements of 25 NZ Battalion began an attempt to systematically clear out a pocket of Germans under Castle Hill, but only managed to eliminate one strongpoint. The major issue facing the New Zealand troops remained the paratroopers holed up in the buildings around the Hotel Continental. What was called for here was a silent night attack by troops skilled in this mode of warfare; the Gurkhas, however, were all up on Hangman's Hill. Instead, 24 NZ Battalion was sent in in a downhill attack in broad daylight. The result, not surprisingly, was a shambles. The survivors of the attack were forced to ground until nightfall, when they were able to make their escape.

Overall it had been a disappointing day. In the end, however, Freyberg decided to send 28 Maori Battalion from 5 NZ Brigade along the axis of Route 6 with the view to cleaning up the Hotel Continental area. As it so happened, discussions between Freyberg and Galloway continued throughout the day and by 7.30pm, in spite of the reverses that day, Galloway had decided that the plan for the monastery attack was acceptable. Nevertheless, he said he would not launch the hook attack by the tanks in the direction of Massa Albaneta unless the attack on the monastery was successful. Freyberg thought the tank attack should go in regardless.[9] Exactly what brought about Freyberg's and Galloway's decision to go ahead with the attack on the monastery and launch Operation Revenge is unclear from these exchanges. To understand this, it is necessary to go a little deeper into the story of the units themselves.

Chapter 10

A Change of Heart

The failure of the New Zealand Division to push through to Phaseline Jockey as planned was not only frustrating for Freyberg and Parkinson, it also proved frustrating for Barton and his squadron. Having set off from San Michele around 4.00pm on 15 March for the area of the barracks, the squadron had difficulty just getting there, the approach road little more than a quagmire thanks to the rain and the shelling. Barton's tanks were forced to retrace their steps and find another way and then, when they eventually reached their jumping-off position, there was further frustration as Barton learned that, after going forward to contact the Indians, they would not be needed that day. In the end they were forced to lie up on the road into the town, the tanks spread out at 100-yard intervals and drawn up close to the side of the road. There the crews had to spend the rest of the day in their tanks, any movement bringing down artillery fire. The most serious incident occurred when Bob Newlands showed up with their rations in a truck that evening. In the ensuing barrage Lieutenant Percy Brooks was killed, along with Corporal Laurie Brenton and their RAP man, Trooper Ray Tollison. Two other men from the squadron were wounded.

More bad news reached Barton the next day. His doubts over the viability of the route they were going to take had prompted the Indians to send a party up the road to check it out and Barton had agreed to send Sergeant Alan Morris. Along with Lieutenant Arthur Murray and accompanied by four Indian sappers from 4 Indian Field Company, Morris had set off on the night of 15/16 March to the castle on Rocca Ianula.[1] Here the group were delayed until Point 165 had been retaken by 1/6 Rajputana Rifles and so Morris and Murray did not get away until 4.00am. and they did so alone as the Indian sappers refused to leave the castle. To defend themselves, all they had was a revolver each and one Thompson sub-machine gun between them. Even then they ran into one of the New Zealand artillery concentrations on Point 165 and had wait for it to lift, losing another hour in the process. They eventually made it to the

The original orders for C Squadron, 20 NZ Armoured Regiment, were for them to drive up the road to the monastery as far as the final stretch below Hangman's Hill and, once there, to provide fire support for the Gurkhas' attack on the monastery. The whole proposal was made impracticable by the German control of the area around the Hotel Continental. (*NARA*)

switchback below Hangman's Hill, finding the road in good repair up to that point – but beyond it they discovered that several craters had made the road impassable and these would have to be filled if the tanks were to make any further progress. It was at around this time that the Gurkhas took Hangman's Hill.

Morris and Murray retraced their steps to Point 202 and then made their way back downhill to look for alternative approaches from Route 6. Heading down the road past the amphitheatre, they struck northwards towards the town but here, with the coming of dawn, they ran into trouble. Seeing the Germans starting to emerge from their defences, they turned to make their way back up the hill. Then a shell landed nearby, forcing them to make a dash into a nearby house that the Germans were using as a store. Here they took shelter in a dugout, with a German they had taken prisoner. Tragedy struck at this point. Morris, while inspecting a passageway leading from the dugout, was killed by a German with a submachine gun. After this, Murray made a break for it, killing a German in another building, before emerging onto the road in front of another thirty of the enemy. Under a hail of fire, he made his getaway, finally reaching Castle Hill that evening.

Losing Morris forced Barton into finding a replacement, and making another hard decision. The only real option was Sergeant Theo Dore, whom Barton had reassigned to his B Echelon after Dore recovered from the injuries suffered at Orsogna, his third wounding since joining the division. As Theo Dore[2] was later to recall:

> I think I was doing that for about a fortnight and Sommerville, who was Major Barton's driver, came in through the gate of this big paddock that we were in and headed straight for us. I felt that the writing was on the wall. I knew what was going to happen. Sure enough he came straight to me and 'Major Barton's in conference here so get your gear and come straight up. Alan Morris was killed last night.'

When Dore rejoined the squadron, he ended up temporarily in charge of his troop.

The news from the reconnaissance by Morris and Murray also brought about a change in orders for Barton, as he later recalled:

> The general plan was that we were to move off about 4.00pm and be in position to move through the town at dawn the following morning, following the 19th Regt. We had an uneventful journey over and waited just short of the town itself. I had a lot of trouble contacting the Indians as it was pitch dark and to add to the joy of the occasion it started to rain. It was obvious that things were going very slowly – the darkness and very rough going was making it terribly difficult for the Indians. We had a certain amount of shelling from a big gun right up on the heights beyond Monte Cairo but suffered no damage that day. When dawn eventually came I moved forward and contacted the 19th Regt Troop who were just in front of us. I went forward with an Engineer officer to have a look at the road and, as we had feared, it was just hopeless – collapsed craters and a sea of mud! I sent most of the squadron back over the causeway as we were getting shelled fairly heavily and reported to Brigade Headquarters that it appeared

hopeless to expect to get through. We waited on call for, I think, another day and then withdrew to an area in olive trees directly opposite Cassino.

* * *

It had been a frustrating time for the men of Major Malcolm Cruickshank's 7 Indian Brigade Recce Squadron and Lieutenant Herman R. Crowder's Company D, 760 Tank Battalion, as their attack was repeatedly delayed. In anticipation of the successful fulfilment of 5 Indian Brigade's side of the plan, they had set off up Cavendish Road on the night of 15/16 March for their respective lying-up areas.[3] The open-topped Indian recce tanks made their way to Madras Circus. Behind them the bulk of the American tanks, after crossing the Rapido, joined up with the Indian Sherman troop and drove up as far as the final bend in the road beyond the two nullahs. The rest of the unit, their supporting M7 HMCs self-propelled guns under Lieutenant Victor F. Hipkiss, and 2 Platoon under 2nd Lieutenant James W. De Right remained down at Caira.[4] The expectation was that by the morning of 16 March tanks from 4 NZ Armoured Brigade and Combat Command B would have broken out into the Liri valley and the Gurkhas would have the monastery firmly in their hands. That would have been the signal to launch the second phase of the plan, Operation Revenge. However, with the failure to achieve either of those, Freyberg had no choice but to postpone the tank thrust. This meant the force on Cavendish Road would have to stay put and, according to Crowder, they were ordered to cover the tanks with camouflage nets. This job was carried out by the Indian engineers with them.

Smokey Edwards was the driver of Lieutenant Wright's tank, along with Girouard the assistant driver and Fullerton the gunner. He later recalled what happened after the camouflage nets were in place:

> That night I was told to set up an outpost with a machine gun and under no circumstance were Germans to come through and find our tanks. It was a cold and frosty night with the moon breaking through the clouds at times. The hills were pretty bare except for clumps of brush and small trees in the draw. Long after dark we could hear a group of Germans, we estimated 10 to 15, coming down the draw 200 to 300 yards away. You could tell them by the sound of their hobnail boots. Our outpost moved out to meet [them] and soon we were in a clump of brush only about 200 feet from them. It was cold and we

could hear one of the Germans snuffling and then his teeth would chatter. After a tense 20 or 30 minutes the Germans withdrew up the draw.[5]

How long the tanks would have remained there on Cavendish Road is not known. On 18 March the war diary of 7 Indian Brigade noted the following:

> 1200 hrs Visited comd 7.I.B., given three alternative plans, A, B, C, told comnd to be by line to Bde HQ if possible and told D day NOT till MONASTERY taken and NZ tanks on Route 6 SW of CASSINO.[6]

However, things changed, as Crowder later noted in connection with the camouflaging:

> This was done very well because we remained undetected for two or three days. Then a lone plane spotted us and we received mild strafing. Fearing the element of surprise had been blown, we made ready to attack the next day. The New Zealanders joined us and the show was on.[7]

Interestingly the situation for Cruickshank also changed, according to his diary entry made two hours later:

> 1400/1630 hrs Visited comd MACOL [Cruickshank] and BARCOL [Barton] and RE. On their return from recce and made rough plan C for co-ordination on 19 Mar. No time for recce; arranged for 19 Mar.
> 1900 hrs CRA [Adye] confirmed Op to start 0600 hrs concurrently with attack on MONASTERY. Confirmed fire plan especially CB on French sector taken and NZ tanks on Route 6 SW of CASSINO.[8]

Another thing had also changed. The inclusion of Barton's C Squadron appeared to have necessitated a change in command and Cruickshank was informed that Lieutenant Colonel John Adye, the Indian Division's acting Commander Royal Artillery (CRA), had been assigned as the force's overall commander.

From the 7 Indian Brigade War Diary it is apparent that Cruickshank was given three possible scenarios to investigate, though it is not clear what all three were. One was the original attack from Madras Circus towards Massa Albaneta. As for one of the others, the idea for it appears to have arisen on 17 March at the headquarters of 4 Indian Division over concern that the Germans might try to withdraw from around the

C Squadron officers photographed in March 1944, prior to the Cavendish Road attack at Cassino. From left to right: Bill de Lautour, Jim Moodie, Pat Barton, Percy Brooks, Jack ('Stuffy') Hazlett, Harold ('Buck') Renall. Hazlett and Renall were both killed during the attack. (*Jim Moodie*)

monastery along the axis Point 575 to Villa San Lucia and that the armoured thrust might come too late to intercept it. This prompted an investigation into an alternative route along the lower slopes on the western side of Monte Castellone to San Lucia. By 6.00pm on 18 March it had become apparent that this alternative was not viable, as aerial photographs indicated that the route would be impassable for tanks.

In the end the original plan was to be followed but the inclusion of the New Zealand squadron had prompted a change for Company D, 760 Tank Battalion. They were now charged with moving up the Castellone feature, destroying Phantom House and exploiting over it in the direction of Villa San Lucia.

If Cruickshank was surprised by this, at least he knew something of the force's objectives, which is more than could be said for Barton, as he later recalled:[9]

> A signal came for Jim [Moodie] and I to report to Brigadier [Oliphant] whose brigade was holding the height above the monastery and right on top of the Jerries. We set off at daybreak and were guided up a

Sergeant Alf Pedder's crew. From left to right: Bill Welch, George Sorich, Alf Pedder, Jack Dasler and Len Gallagher. Sorich and Dasler leapt out of their tank at Massa Albaneta and took shelter in a bomb crater. Their bodies were discovered there after the battle. (*Peter Scott*)

most precipitous track and arrived very out of breath to be presented with bacon and eggs by the Brigadier. The HQ was in an old farmhouse from which there was a truly magnificent view of the whole valley. Jerry must have been very short of ammo because we could see all our own positions as plain as daylight. The Brig then gave us the 'oil'. There was a plan to make a diversion with a squadron of tanks from [Caira] by means of a road which had just been completed – the general idea being to attack along towards Albaneta House while an infantry attack was launched from Hangman's Hill. There were to be no infantry with us as they were thin on the ground and could not spare a man. There would be about six or eight Yank 'Honey' tanks and a troop of Shermans from a Hussar regiment. We would be under the command of an English colonel. We were told it would not be possible to launch the attack for three or four days at least. Captain Moodie and I were then taken on a recce of the possible routes we would take. We crawled on our stomachs to OPs all day and had a most interesting if strenuous day. We had a good recce of the ground but, of course, could not tell just what the 'going' was like.

We finished by visiting the French Brigade HQ and several of their OPs. The Free French were most bloodthirsty gentlemen and had a most endearing habit of pointing to the Jerry lines and slowly drawing a hand across their throats. We were thankful they were on our side. We finished by walking down the road where the Yank and British tanks were – met the CO Col. [Adye] and the Tommy commander Maj. Cruickshank. They had been there for several days under enormous camouflage nets. We finally arrived at the spot where we had left Slim Sommerville with the jeep, about 6.00pm. Slim was most irate as he had been subjected to three air raids, which had not pleased him at all. When we got back the squadron was quite convinced we had either been captured, killed or both.

It was late to have a conference then and my information was very vague in any case so I told the troop commanders to be ready to go and look at the route in the morning and then left to see Brigadier Stewart at 4 Bde. There were several aspects of the show which I did not like – no infantry, little artillery support, a rather vague objective and a CO who had never had any experience with tanks at all. Brig. Stewart did not like the scheme any more than I did and rang up Corps. You can imagine my astonishment when they said the show was starting at 6.00am the next morning! Here was I, 15 miles from the squadron, who were all blissfully asleep! It was one of those moments I wished I was on Brigade HQ. Slim and I dashed madly back to our area and found no word of a move at all. I hopefully thought that there might be some mistake and went to 6 Bde HQ where, after a lot of trouble, I managed to contact the Indians who said that Col. [Adye] was on his way down to see me. To this day I cannot imagine why no attempt was made to contact us and give us some warning. If I had not gone to 4 Bde that would have been our first news of the attack. As you can imagine, our comments on the higher command were not flattering. Everyone was aroused and a hurried conference held by candlelight and the troop commanders given the meagre information. I had reckoned on an hour at least to make the move from our area to the top of the hill. Col. [Adye] eventually arrived about 1.30am. We had another conference – our orders were to capture Albaneta House and exploit towards the monastery if it was thought possible. The biggest setback was that Col. [Adye] had no direct communication back with 4th Indian Div. and had to have another No. 19 set put in the tank in which he was.

The Chiesa del Carmine (The Convent), pictured on 12 April 1944.

Barton arranged for Ray Hodge from EME to install this radio set in Sergeant Owen Hughes' tank of 9 Troop, C Squadron, forcing Hughes to command his tank from the spare driver's position. This was all done at night with no lights showing.

Chapter 11

Cavalry Ride to Albaneta

After three days of inactivity, the Indian and US tanks finally got going and drove up the remaining part of the road in the early hours of 19 March. In the lead were the three Shermans and five Stuarts from the Recce Squadron and the seventeen Stuarts from Company D, followed by Hipkiss' M7 HMCs. Also with them was 12 Indian Field Company with a D-7 tractor and two D-6 bulldozers – which were shortly to prove their worth. Near the top of the road, Sergeant Carrigan's Sherman from the Indian Recce Squadron had problems with a slipping clutch, holding them up for half an hour. In the end his tank had to be towed to the top by one of the D-6 bulldozers.[1]

Further back were Barton's sixteen Shermans from C Squadron. They had set off from their lying-up area at around 4.30am, travelling nose to tail all the way. Their first casualty was Corporal Rex Miller's Sherman from No. 9 Troop, as he recalled:

> I was in the very last tank. That was rather fortunate, had it not been for that it would have held up the whole thing because it would have been difficult for anything to get past it; [it] part blocked the road. The previous tanks had slightly damaged the edge of the road. By the time we got there it wouldn't take any more. It just gave away and over we went. We were there for a few days. We couldn't get the tank out, we had to just wait and see what happened. We might have been very unlucky, if we had gone another way over it would have killed the lot of us because it was a long steep slope down to a gulley below us. It would have rolled down there; inside a tank you wouldn't have survived.[2]

Miller's spare driver Allan Coleman put down his thoughts later in a letter:[3]

> We were the last tank in the convoy and somewhere along the road the right-hand side of the track gave way and we finished up at about

The first casualty of C Squadron, 20 NZ Armoured Regiment, was Corporal Rex Miller's Sherman III from No. 9 Troop. It slipped off the road from Caira on the way up to Cavendish Road. Fortunately it was the last tank in the line and did not block the others. (*Polish Institute and Sikorski Museum*)

> a 45 degree angle with one track off. Miller had us immediately cover the tank with the camouflage net. It was by then breaking day and we could listen in to the squadron on the radio.

The rest of the squadron ran into problems with the camouflage nets that had been erected along the part of the road that was visible to the Germans. According to Captain Jim Moodie, the squadron battle captain:[4]

> Camouflage nets, making a sort of tunnel, hundreds of yards after hundreds of yards after hundreds of yards and the stuff would get caught in the radio aerials, the flaps of the turret flaps ...

Len Gallagher, the spare driver in Sergeant Alf Pedder's tank in 11 Troop, recalled another problem experienced by the column on their way up:

> The track was steep and just wide enough to take a tank. We were held up for a while owing to some of the tanks having trouble with water in the fuel.[5]

By the time they all reached Madras Circus at 7.30am, it was daylight. Here the tanks halted, as Moodie related:

> There we met a company of Essex infantry, British infantry. And they stabilised the base as infantry. They dug in there and they were token defence against us being overrun.

The original plan was still supposed to be in force and the tanks were not to advance until they had received word that the monastery had been captured. Unfortunately, things had not been going well over there. The Essex troops had set out from Castle Hill as ordered, two companies reaching the Gurkhas on Hangman's Hill without incident. However, the other two companies, halfway up, noticed some German troops moving down towards the castle and quickly retraced their steps. It was not a moment too soon. The German attackers fell first upon the troops at Point 165, overwhelming them, before turning their attention to the castle itself. Savage fighting ensued. Although the Germans were repulsed, they came on again at 7.30am and the battle continued until 9.30, when their attack faltered and finally ceased.

These attacks effectively put paid to any thoughts of launching the Gurkhas and Essex against the monastery but with the tanks having successfully traversed Cavendish Road and ready to go Freyberg decided to launch Revenge anyway. Accordingly, Crowder's tanks led off from Madras Circus, up the valley and through the first 'bottleneck', a narrow point in the valley where a spur ran down from Phantom Ridge.[6] Here 3 Platoon, under 2nd Lieutenant John A. Crews, proceeded up towards Phantom House, a house in front of the French lines that was being used as a German observation post. Here the terrain was steeply terraced and one Stuart threw a track. Crew's platoon then made another attempt with 1 Platoon but three more Stuarts lost their tracks in the attempt, including Crews' own tank. Floyd Snyder was in one of the tanks:

> We hit a mine and it knocked a track off. We sat there all day and that night we got out. Hutchinson came in in an armoured vehicle and got us out. It had been a rough day. There were snipers after us all the time.[7]

It was around this time that Lieutenant James W. De Right's 2 Platoon and Hipkiss' M7 HMCs moved into covering positions and all but levelled Phantom House with shell-fire. Lieutenant Chester M. Wright then went

The ruins of 'Phantom House' after it had been 'done over' by Lieutenant Victor F. Hipkiss' 105mm Howitzer Motor Carriage M7s. At least one battle report described this as being a blockhouse but it is apparent that it was just an ordinary Italian farmhouse, although almost certainly it had been strengthened in normal German fashion through the use of railway sleepers or similar. (*Polish Institute and Sikorski Museum*)

One of the M5A1 Light Tanks from Company D, 760 Tank Battalion, became bogged just beyond Hazlett's Sherman III. (*Polish Institute and Sikorski Museum*)

Company D had to abandon several M5A1 Light Tanks after they got stuck in soft ground while trying to attack Phantom House. The Germans blew them up later. (*Polish Institute and Sikorski Museum*)

forward on foot to determine if a way could be found to Phantom House, presumably with the view to seeing if they could carry out the second phase of the operation and exploiting towards Villa San Lucia. Unsuccessful in this venture, he returned to his tank. At this point the company abandoned the endeavour and turned back up the valley to rendezvous with the rest of the force. Crowder also ran into difficulties. The radio transmitter in his tank failed and he was forced to transfer to one of the open-topped Indian Recce Stuarts.[8]

Barton's squadron set off shortly after the Americans with orders to 'try to get Shermans onto [the] monastery area as soon as possible'.[9] With Second Lieutenant Jack ('Stuffy') Hazlett's 11 Troop in the lead, they drove up a grassy valley between rough, bush-covered hills, sown with anti-personnel Shu-mines, which went off under their tracks like firecrackers. Within a few minutes, Hazlett's tank slipped off the road and into a small ditch. With no way of recovering it, Hazlett switched to Sergeant Alf Pedder's tank and carried on.[10] This was not the squadron's only casualty. Sergeant Owen Hughes' tank with Colonel Adye on board (which was

Pushing on from Madras Circus, three of the New Zealand Shermans soon became disabled in the rough going, including no. 9 from No. 11 Troop, under the command of Second Lieutenant 'Stuffy' Hazlett, which slipped into this small ditch.
(*Polish Institute and Sikorski Museum*)

trying to set up a command post at Phantom House) ran off its tracks, as did Sergeant Major Jock Laidlaw's Sherman from Squadron Headquarters. Adye transferred to another tank from the Indian Recce squadron. Efforts were made to recover Laidlaw's tank using a bulldozer but came under mortar and small arms fire and the attempt was abandoned.

Shortly after Hazlett's tank capsized, Lieutenant Bill de Lautour's tank shed a track trying to climb a spur on Phantom Ridge. It appears to have been demolished by the Germans after the battle. (*Polish Institute and Sikorski Museum*)

According to Barton, Laidlaw was furious beyond belief. Barton's tank nearly succumbed as well:[11]

> My own tank got bogged and if it had not been for some masterly driving by Trooper George Hanrahan we would have been there yet.

The next casualty was Second Lieutenant Bill de Lautour's Sherman, which shed a track trying to climb a rocky spur on Phantom Ridge, from where he was hoping to give covering fire. He transferred to his troop sergeant's tank.

The Indians also lost a Sherman when it became grounded in a bomb crater.[12] Their efforts to string a phone line up to a company from 1 Royal Sussex Regiment, at that time occupying some of the French FDLs, were also unsuccessful. They managed to reel a line through to Phantom Ridge but a mortar burst carried the line away, the tank commander being wounded by shrapnel from another mortar burst in the process. In the end they decided to fall back on the radio net for communication, controlling both the Recce Squadron and C Squadron through the tank of Barton's second-in-command.

At this stage the only opposition they had encountered was from a few infantry as Hipkiss's Priests had effectively knocked out the OP at Phantom House.[13] In fact things were looking favourable enough for 4 Indian Division Headquarters to consider releasing a company from 1 Royal Sussex to support the tanks, though took the matter no further.

After passing through a narrow defile by way of the track, about 300 yards from their start line, Jim Moodie encountered his first German:[14]

> The first surprise was the surprise from us. I was in about the third or fourth tank going towards the monastery after Madras Circus in a rut that tank tracks make in softish ground and along came a wounded German soldier carrying a wee white flag, crawling along towards us. This was the 1st German Parachute Division. Of course you don't fluff around with guys crawling anywhere, you carry on. Infantry will get them, [but] of course we had no infantry you see.

Following the New Zealand tanks, Smokey Edwards witnessed one of them catch fire:

> When we finally moved up the hill with our tank we ran into a lot of anti-personnel mines. No anti-tank mines since the Germans never expected tanks there. We watched the New Zealand tank ahead of us

getting caught by mortar fire, which set their camouflage net aflame. They finally dropped it off.[15]

The tank in question was Jim Moodie's, one round setting on fire the gear strapped to the back of it. It could have ended badly but for an American in one of the open-topped Honey tanks, as Moodie recalled:[16]

> So, speak of the devil, we go another few hundred yards and [I] got a smack in the back of the head. We had some light Yank Honey tanks in the rougher ground on our flanks. We were getting along, we were being shelled at this stage, pretty heavily, I had my head down in the turret and you're playing catch me and I got a slap on the back of the head. I looked up and here's an American soldier leaning over me. I pulled off the headphones and he said: 'Say, Captain, I guess your tank's on fire.' I looked around and [there] was a roaring sheet of flame, so there you are. If it was good enough for him to come across about 50 yards from his Honey to tell me the tank was on fire, it was good enough for me to get out, against every instinct. You're in enemy territory now, scrub and rock, paratroopers. He gives me the extinguisher. So I gave it a squirt and the extinguisher it sends a white squirt [only so] far then dissipates. It didn't go anywhere near the rear end of the tank. So I get out and get the extinguisher and get up the rear of the tank and got the extinguisher close enough to squirt and kick off any rubbish and got back in the tank without being shot.

Smokey Edwards was also witness to one of the more bizarre events in the attack:

> At mid-morning the New Zealanders stopped for tea right where they were. They were cooking their tea on the rear deck of their tank when a bullet went through the pot. They spotted the sniper and with a cry of: 'The bloody bloke shot our tea pot', they wheeled the turret and fired a round.[17]

With Second Lieutenant Harold ('Buck') Renall's troop in the lead, they forced their way up to the second of the two single-track defiles, known more generally as 'the Bottleneck', where Renall and his troop found themselves on a saddle overlooking Massa Albaneta, which lay a little below them on a flat plateau. Corporal Dick Jones in Renall's troop recalled:[18]

> Buck called (on the wireless) to say that we would advance to Albaneta House in two-up formation, covering the left scrubby

hillside while Jack Hazlett looked after our right with his troop. Our 'two-up' consisted of Buck and myself forward with covering fire from our sergeant's tank. We decided to advance 'leap-frogging' each other with approximately 300-yard bounds, each giving covering fire in turn. Here we found for the first time how vulnerable a tank is on the move in rough going. I tried at first to secure hull-down positions at the end of each advance, but soon gave up this idea as we nearly got stuck twice, and anyway our advance was much quicker than we anticipated.

Just as Buck gave the word to move, a German crawled out of the scrub waving a white flag. Here I think if we had infantry we could have captured many prisoners as they were starting to appear everywhere, but just then our covering tanks were through and opened up.

As we leap-frogged our way forward it became obvious that we had caught Jerry napping. Just through the gap Buck wiped out a machine-gun nest, the Germans bravely firing away at us until the end. All the way we pounded the hillside and I think we must have inflicted heavy casualties as we could pick up a good few Germans moving about.

As we advanced up the plateau we were all conscious of a narrow part, and my crew knew as well as I that if Jerry had anything heavy in the 'Nunnery' [Massa Albaneta] we would be a sitting shot. With the way our advance had gone, it was our tank's turn to advance first through the 'bottleneck', as Buck and I had been calling it.

As we prepared to advance through I told our driver, Jack Hodge, to drive as fast as possible, swerving from side to side. Buck opened up on Albaneta House and Jack Hazlett's troop was also concentrating on it. When it was practically obscured by dust we moved. In the turret we tossed about as the tank swerved and bucked. I am sure we all held our breath in spite of this. When we stopped Steve Lewis, our gunner, opened up on the 'Nunnery' with AP and HE, while Joe Costello, our spare driver, raked it with his .30 Browning, much to his delight. Buck moved through while we kept up the bombardment.

Beyond this point was a steep gully to the west ('Death Gully') and the Liri valley. Here the advance started to come under heavy artillery fire. While the rest of the squadron gathered on the crest, Renall's troop proceeded down the track, followed by Hazlett's two tanks, the latter with orders to cover Massa Albaneta. Barton, however, kept Sergeant Theo

Dore back with the words: 'Don't you go down there, Dore.'[19] Eventually the tanks rounded the southern shoulder of Point 593 and disappeared from sight. It was at this point that things started to go wrong as resistance from the Germans hardened. Hazlett's tank, the first casualty, was hit by a mortar round, as Jones describes:[20]

> It was at this time I realised that our ammunition was running low. Our Browning tins were nearly empty and our 75mm bins were getting bare. Every shot had to count now.
>
> We turned left and went forward a hundred yards or so and somebody on the air said to 'put out that fire on that tank'. While I was looking around to see if it was ours, I saw the camouflage net on Jack's tank on fire and Jack [Hazlett] climbing out to extinguish it. Seconds later he fell off the tank.

Len Gallagher wrote about it later in his diary:

> We put a few AP rounds in the Nunnery and some HE in some little houses up the gully. We were then called up over the air and told that our tank was on fire. Stuffy got out with a fire extinguisher and immediately there was a rat-tat of Spandau and Stuffy was killed. We made for the shelter of the Nunnery and then there was a burst of flame in the turret. Jack Dasler and George Sorich then bailed out and Bill Welch and I got out through the escape hatch. Bill stopped the engines and pulled the fire extinguisher levers before he got [out]. Prior to that Bill noticed a flash from a window in the Nunnery and at the same time a mortar bomb hit in front and smashed the periscopes and blew my hatch open.[21]

Corporal Reg Lennie, from their troop, followed them over but his tank took a round from a Panzerschreck (a German version of the American bazooka) that disabled one of his motors. They then attempted to pull out in the tank but slipped over into a shell hole in the flat by the building.

Next Renall's luck ran out, as Trooper Frank Brice, his gunner, was later to recall in a letter:[22]

> There was a gap we had to go through. On the right was a German gun position. We did that over. We then carried on over to the 'Nunnery' [Massa Albaneta]. Did that over. We were told to move on which we did. We had not gone very far when I could hear bullets hitting the side of the turret.

Corporal Reg Lennie's Sherman III after it slipped sideways into a ditch on the flat by Massa Albaneta, while trying to rejoin the rest of the force. He and his crew were later rescued by American and Indian tanks. (*Polish Institute and Sikorski Museum*)

Buck [Renall], who had part of his head out of the turret, could not make this out. I said to him to keep his head down or he would get 'it'. He put his hand on my shoulder and said 'Frank, we were told that we held all that side of the slope which was covered in scrub.' Next we moved on and could see the back of the monastery.

There was a gap of about 20 yards and we could see Germans running across and down a steep hill. Just before this, not five minutes, Buck fell on top of me, he had been shot through the side of his head. From then on we couldn't do much as I was busy with holding Buck. We had to retreat to our start point to get Buck out.

We seemed to be under mortar fire all the time.

We heard over the wireless that a fire had started on the back of a tank, I think it was Stuffy Hazlett's tank. He was told to put it out. That put the tank out of action and of course he was killed.

After getting Buck out, on checking around, we found that our own radiator was leaking so that put us out of action.

Finally Dick Jones' tank was penetrated by a round from a Panzerschreck:

> We advanced another stage to the left but shortage of ammunition didn't allow us to do the hill [Point 593] on the left over as thoroughly as we had on our advance ... I moved a bit further to get a better view of the track to the monastery and the shelling was terrific. We nearly got stuck, only superb driving by Jack Hodge got us out.
>
> Word came that Buck was killed. I realised that our reconnaissance would have to be quick as we couldn't fire our 75mm much and our Browning (co-ax.) was terribly hot and wasting ammunition by 'running away', in spite of the oil which Steve threw on it.
>
> It was while looking at the possible route that we got hit.
>
> Regaining consciousness, I saw that my arm was bleeding badly and must have a tourniquet quickly. I looked up to see Joe Costello gazing through the turret at me. How he wasn't hit is a mystery. Steve was slumped over his 75mm bleeding badly from his back and head. Tom Middleton was lying on the floor, having fallen off the seat by his wireless. With difficulty I managed to traverse the turret by hand to allow Jack to scramble through to apply the tourniquet.
>
> This applied, I told Jack to try the motors. It was with a prayer on our lips he pressed the starter. The left engine roared into life to be followed by the right immediately afterwards. With his head out of the driver's hatch, the better to see and get maximum speed, Jack

drove out through our own tanks, which were still pounding away at the enemy, to the forward CCS.[23]

While the battered tanks rallied back to the saddle overlooking Massa Albaneta, their commanders were taking stock of the situation. By now it was becoming obvious that their main problem was Point 593. Here the German paratroopers in their camouflaged uniforms were well hidden among the scrub that clung to the slopes above them. They were hard to locate and even harder to hit, but their persistent, accurate sniping was forcing the tank commanders to keep their heads inside their turrets with only the briefest look outside. They could keep the heads of the Germans down with machine-gun fire but what was really needed was some infantry of their own to secure the ground around them. Unfortunately, that was not forthcoming.

Freyberg was still hopeful of launching the Gurkhas against the monastery, if this entry in 4 Indian Division Headquarters diary, made during the drive of Renall's and Hazlett's troops, is anything to go by:[24]

> GOC's note. At 1055 hrs information received that the t[an]ks of REVENGE were reported by RA OP 31 F[iel]d past ALBANET[A] House heading for MONASTERY. Discussed Corps Comd and following agreed:- (a) if tks reach sufficiently close to MONASTERY to make contact feasible, force on HANGMAN'S HILL will be ordered to attack MONASTERY under cover of bombardment and join up with tks. (b) if (a) not feasible, then I will not contemplate any attack on MONASTERY or any increase of forces in the hills (with that object in view) until the supply situation secure and CASSINO cleared up properly. (c) Under (b) above 193 to be secured against possibility of capture, 165 recaptured and secured and steps taken to prevent infiltration down RAVINE into CASSINO.

From this, it is apparent that an artillery spotter plane flying over the area at the time must have sighted Renall's and Jones' tanks in their push past Massa Albaneta. Based on this sighting, 4 Indian Division Headquarters had decided (on consultation with NZ Corps HQ) to reprise the Gurkha/Essex attack on the monastery from Hangman's Hill.

Nevertheless there were still some doubts as to the feasibility of this, as this diary entry timed at 11.15am indicates:[25]

> Com[man]d 7 Bde to G.I. Tks have been round to ALBANET house for some time. Believe NZ tks are going along a track via Pt 444

towards MONASTERY. Comm with leading t[roo]p now blacked out. Doubtful if they can join up with 1/9 GR [Gurkha Rifles] in latter's present posn therefore inf[antry] will have to come up and meet them. Alternatively might try to send tks down NORTH side of Pt 445 wadi. Trying to contact REVENGE Comd (at present off the air) and will keep us informed.

Back at the saddle overlooking Massa Albaneta it was midday and the force had now been on the saddle above their objective for some three hours. Worse still, Barton was now seven tanks down, not counting the two on the flats by Massa Albaneta, and the Americans had lost four tanks. Barton contacted the force commander, seeking further orders. With the attack from Hangman's Hill now apparently impracticable and no infantry available to hold the ground they had taken, Adye's initial response was to order them to rally back to Madras Circus. However, this was countermanded by 7 Indian Brigade Headquarters after Cruickshank, not knowing Adye's intentions, queried these orders with his HQ. The desire to push on to the monastery was still there but by 12.20pm they appeared to be losing heart over this move:[26]

> G.II to 7 Bde. Flying OP reports that leading tks still 200yds short of ALBANET house. Comd 7 Bde says no more from tks for some time except for intercepted message order rally back to MADRAS CIRCUS which has been countermanded.

Another entry a few minutes later read:

> Comd 7 Bde to G.I. Six tks now fwd to ALBANET HOUSE finding going bad on one tank front.

The next entry, timed at 12.45pm, made it clear what the problem was:

> GOC's Note. Spoke Comd 7 Bde who said that tk force Comd had got past ALBANET HOUSE, had reported it impossible to get on towards MONASTERY except on a one tk front and <u>then</u> only if considerable RE work was done. This, under hy mortar and MG fire which this force was subjected to, was not possible. Told Comd 7 Bde <u>that he had exhausted every possibility of getting</u> on to MONASTERY if he could not get on, then he would have to get his tk force back to the CIRCUS before dark, secure from attack by enemy inf at night, re-fuelled etc. and ready to function again next day.

With the higher echelons of command apparently paralysed by indecision and no further orders to go on, Barton turned his attention to rescuing the crews of the two tanks on the flats below.[27] One of his problems was solved without him doing anything, as Len Gallagher later wrote:

> We lay underneath the tank and considered the best way out. The box of Browning .30 on the back was alight and the rounds were going off. I saw a chap running and get into a tank and thought that George and Jack had been picked up. Then Bill saw something moving in this window, which was covered with a bit of sacking and I thought our number was up. Either they did not see us under the tank or they were afraid to open fire for fear of betraying their position. Bill de Lautour came up in his tank and poured HE into the window. I had a look inside the tank and fire appeared to be going out so I tried the motors. They started alright and the fuel and oil seemed OK on the gauge. I called Bill inside and I tried to get into the turret but could not move it but placed the lever in the free position. We then backed out and turned around. I kept an eye out for Jack and George but could not see any sign of them so we carried on out. The turret swung around and I was able to get in. The wireless was out of action and then I noticed a hole under the 75 gun the size of a .50 and the projectile had broken the oil pipe from the traversing gear motor and pump. We pulled up just out a little bit and took stock of things. Bob Guthrie's tank then pulled alongside and I saw a hole in his side by the RH fuel tank. He said he had fuel out all over the floor of the tank and that shrapnel had pierced his radiators and one engine was thereby out of action. We were getting shelled and mortared so moved on down to an area near the Sgt Major's tank.[28]

According to Gallagher, they then drove back to Madras Circus:

> We stayed down there for the rest of the day. We had a lot of shit slung at us but no direct hits though sprayed with shrapnel. Jerry planes were over and one bomb dropped near us. Towards dark the other tanks came out, some with radiators pierced. About 6 o'clock I was told I was being sent back and went down to the top of the road, 9 of us.[29]

Other tanks from the squadron tried to put down smoke to help Lennie's crew make a dash for it, as the sniping was severe, but Major Barton was reluctant to send down another of his tanks to rescue them as by then he only had five runners available to him. So, as covering fire was laid down by the other tanks, Lieutenant Chester M. Wright in his Stuart and one of the Indian tanks raced in and got the men to safety, carrying them out on their engine decks.[30] The tanks then settled down where they were to await further orders, though not for long. At 2.20pm an intercept of a German radio transmission was received at Freyberg's headquarters:[31]

> From Comms Comd. Enemy states (Y Intercept) that eight tks (REVENGE) have broken through his main line and that an inf attack seems probable at any time. Tell 7 Bde that this is good work and to keep up their show with those tks.

This time, however, there was to be a slight change of approach, according to Freyberg's post-battle report:[32]

> The track was so narrow and the ground either side so rough and steep that the tanks were obliged to follow each other in single file; the going was too rough for Shermans; moreover, the track was mined. Comd 7 Indian Inf Bde was obliged to report that considerable engineer work was needed before the tanks could reach the monastery and this was impossible because the track was under heavy fire from mortars and machine-guns. He was told by GOC 4 Indian Div to exhaust every possibility of getting on then, if unsuccessful, to withdraw the force to Madras Circus before dark and prepare to renew the attempt the next day. In the hope that the light tanks would be able to negotiate the rough ground better, the heavy column was withdrawn and the light column sent forward.

It may have been pure coincidence but shortly after this Revenge Force was galvanised into action, the task falling this time on Crowder's shoulders.

Unfortunately, while the higher command had been dithering over what to do next, the Germans had not. The noise of the approaching tanks was only too evident to the Germans and word soon got back to Major Franz Grassmehl, the acting commander of Fallschirmjäger-Regiment 4. He had no hesitation in sending a party of pioneers up Death Gully from Route 6 with anti-tank and other weapons. Among them was Bob Frettlohr:[33]

> One morning when the tanks came through an alarm went off. The Leutnant said: 'Get ready, get all your [anti-]tank equipment. We're

going up to Albaneta Farm. The English have broken through with Sherman tanks.' We said: 'Through where, there isn't a road or anything.' So we set off to go up to Albaneta Farm but we had a hell of a job to get up there because we were sighted in by the Allied artillery on various points. I eventually made it up to there but the battle was already on with the tanks. There was a tank already in flames. There were a few stuck there. We had all our anti-tank gear so went right back and sealed off an area [with mines] where they [might] try to push through again.

Grassmehl also ordered forward the commander of the regiment's 14.(Panzerjäger-)Kompanie, Oberleutnant Raimund Eckel, to investigate. As it so happened, he was in the command post of II. Batallion in a cave between Massa Albaneta and the monastery at the time.[34]

Around 3.30pm Crowder from Company D, 760 Tank Battalion, sent 1 Platoon under 2nd Lieutenant Chester M. Wright and the first section of 3 Platoon under Crews around towards the monastery in single file.[35] Smokey Edwards was among them:

> As we passed over a ridge we suddenly found that we could see up the valley to the north and see the flash of German artillery. We turned left along a narrow stone road and as we rounded a bend we ran into a company of Germans coming up the road. We opened fire with everything we had with Lieutenant Wright's first section of three tanks, while Sergeant Custer and the other two moved into position.[36]

Then, on the flats below, they spread out. Unfortunately ahead of them were Eckel and Gefreiter Kammermann armed with a Panzerschreck:[37]

> Carefully, making use of every scrap of available cover the three men advanced like stalkers towards Albaneta, 300 yards away. From the shelter of a rock they suddenly caught sight of a number of enemy tanks, rattling along a narrow mountain path.

According to Paratrooper Werner Eggert at this stage one tank (Crews') was out in front of the rest of the tanks:

> As I was about to leave for the command post the shooting started. I found cover behind the walls of our waterhole. The tanks approached in a keel line and were indeed without accompanying infantry. The first one made it through just about to where I was ... he noticed his

Oberleutnant Raimund Eckel and Karl Newedel. (*Karl Newedel*)

The first casualty of the American thrust towards the monastery was M5A1 *Dead Eye Dick*, commanded by Second Lieutenant John A. Crews, which was hit by a round from Jäger Kammermann's Panzerschreck as it was trying to turn around and rejoin the other tanks. (*NARA*)

> isolation, when he tried to turn and he was suddenly fired at out of an *ofenrohr* [Panzerschreck].[38]

This was Kammerman and Eckel's weapon:

> Calmly Kammermann took aim and pressed the trigger. Misfire! The second round was also a misfire. He now had only one round left; if that failed, the golden opportunity would be lost. But this time, the shot, well and truly aimed, hit the tank, which burst into flames. Three of the tanks now turned in the direction of the monastery. On that course, Eckel rightly foresaw, they would be confined to a narrow hill path, the steep sides of which precluded any possibility of deviation. Eckel set off in pursuit. He had no short-range anti-tank weapon, but he hoped he might be able to lob a grenade into an open turret. But when his party were close to Albaneta, they found, quite by accident, three T-mines. That was indeed a find, and it did not take

Eckel long to make up his mind how to use them. Hastening forward at their best speed on the flank of the tanks, the little party managed to get sufficiently ahead on the flank of them to enable them to plant the mines on the hill path.[39]

As luck would have it, the next tank under Staff Sergeant Lawrence R. Custer, after pushing past Crews' disabled tank, ran onto one of the mines and had a track blown off. The crew continued to engage the enemy troops in the area, prompting Eckel to attack the tank again; using a rifle grenade as a hand grenade, he put its hull machine gun out of action. With nothing left to fight with, Eckel went in search of something he could use against the tanks. Fortunately he knew where there was a store of mines so he headed off in that direction.

With Custer's tank effectively blocking the road, and particularly with German troops in close proximity, efforts turned to rescuing the crews of the stricken tanks.[40] Smokey Edwards was involved in one attempt:

> We had to pull back over the hill under heavy fire from the valley below. My tank tracks were severely damaged and I had to switch to another tank to go back after Custer. He was busy firing at the enemy and asked us to pull back.[41]

Crowder came forward in the Indian recce tank that he had transferred to and pulled up beside Custer's Stuart. They managed to transfer Custer and his assistant driver, Private Floyd Snyder, to their tank but, realising that there were a number of Germans in the area, Crowder ordered his other tanks to pull back. Despite this order, Staff Sergeant John Kovak came forward in his tank and pulled alongside Custer's vehicle. At that point they realised that they were surrounded on three sides by paratroopers and backed off. One of the men left behind in the tank was Doyle Cox:

> I was the driver in the lead tank. We made it without much trouble until we got almost to the last curve from the monastery. I hit a mine with the left track, which put us out [of action]. The tank behind threw out smoke grenades to cover us and the lieutenant and assistant driver got out and into the tank behind us and were taken back.

(**Opposite & following**) Sergeant Lawrence R. Custer then passed Crew's stricken tank in his M5A1, *Devil's Playmate*, but ran onto a mine laid by Oberleutnant Raimund Eckel, which blew the left track off. Custer and his spare driver escaped at this point and were rescued, but the other two were captured before Eckel returned with more mines and destroyed the tank. (*Polish Institute and Sikorski Museum*)

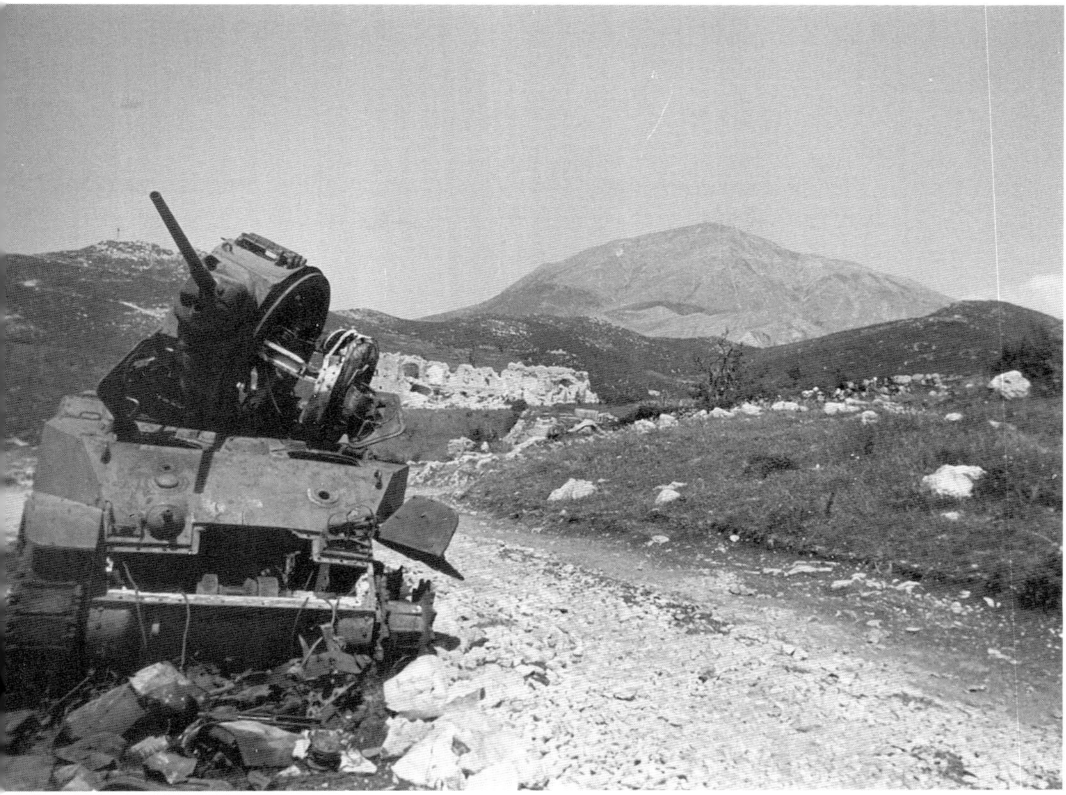

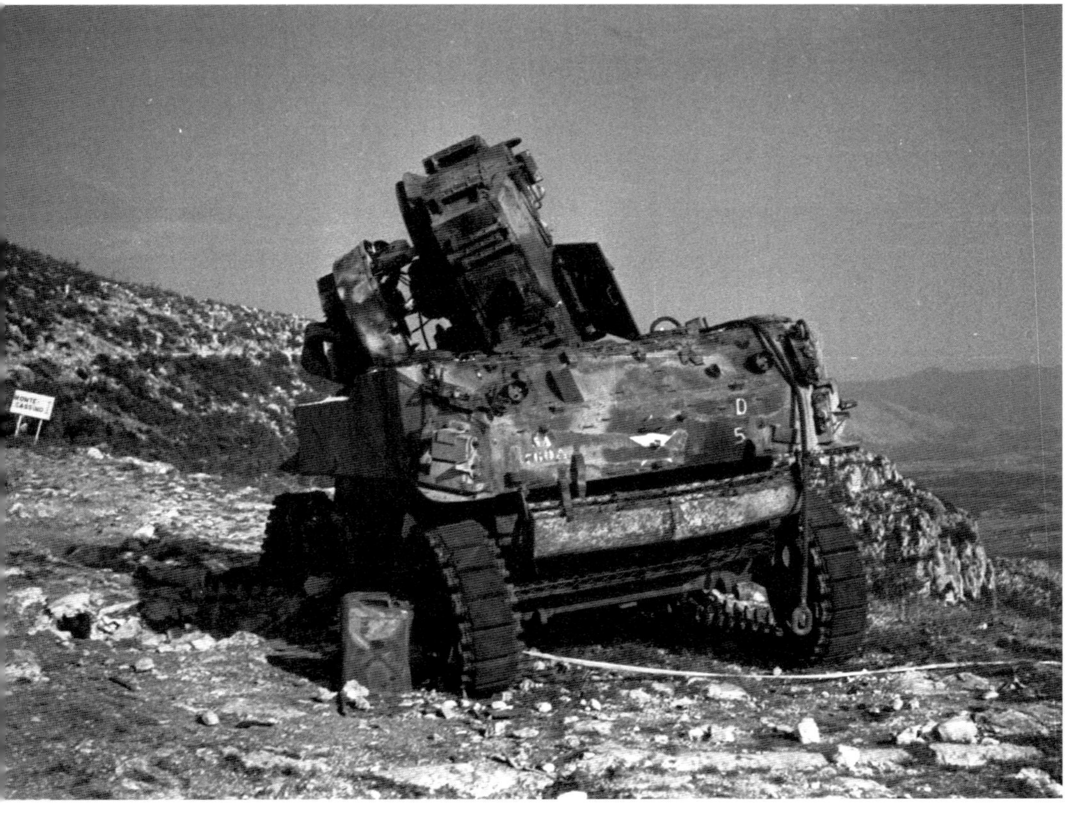
D
5

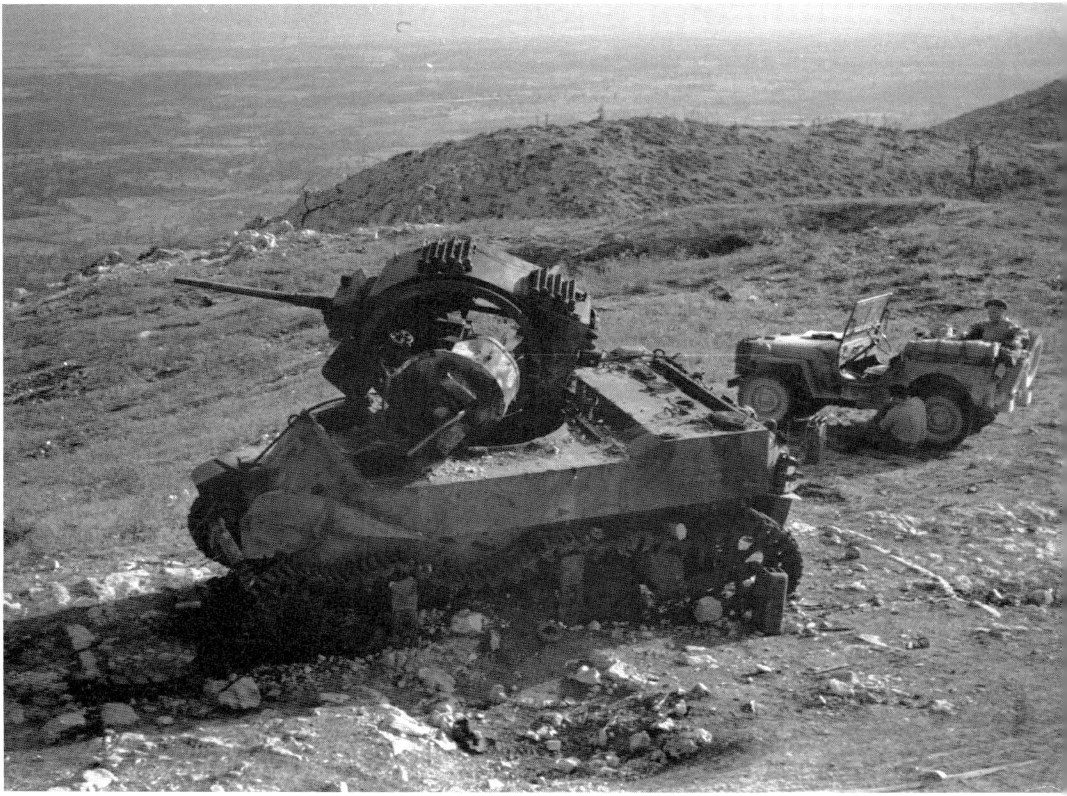

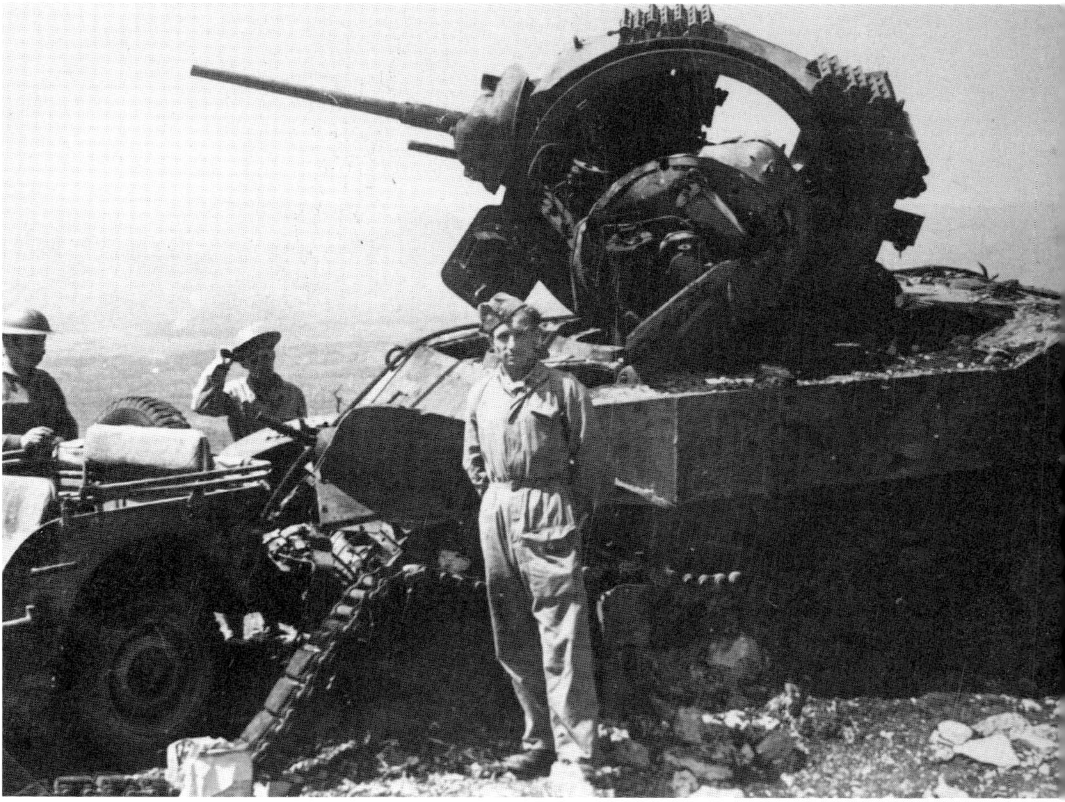

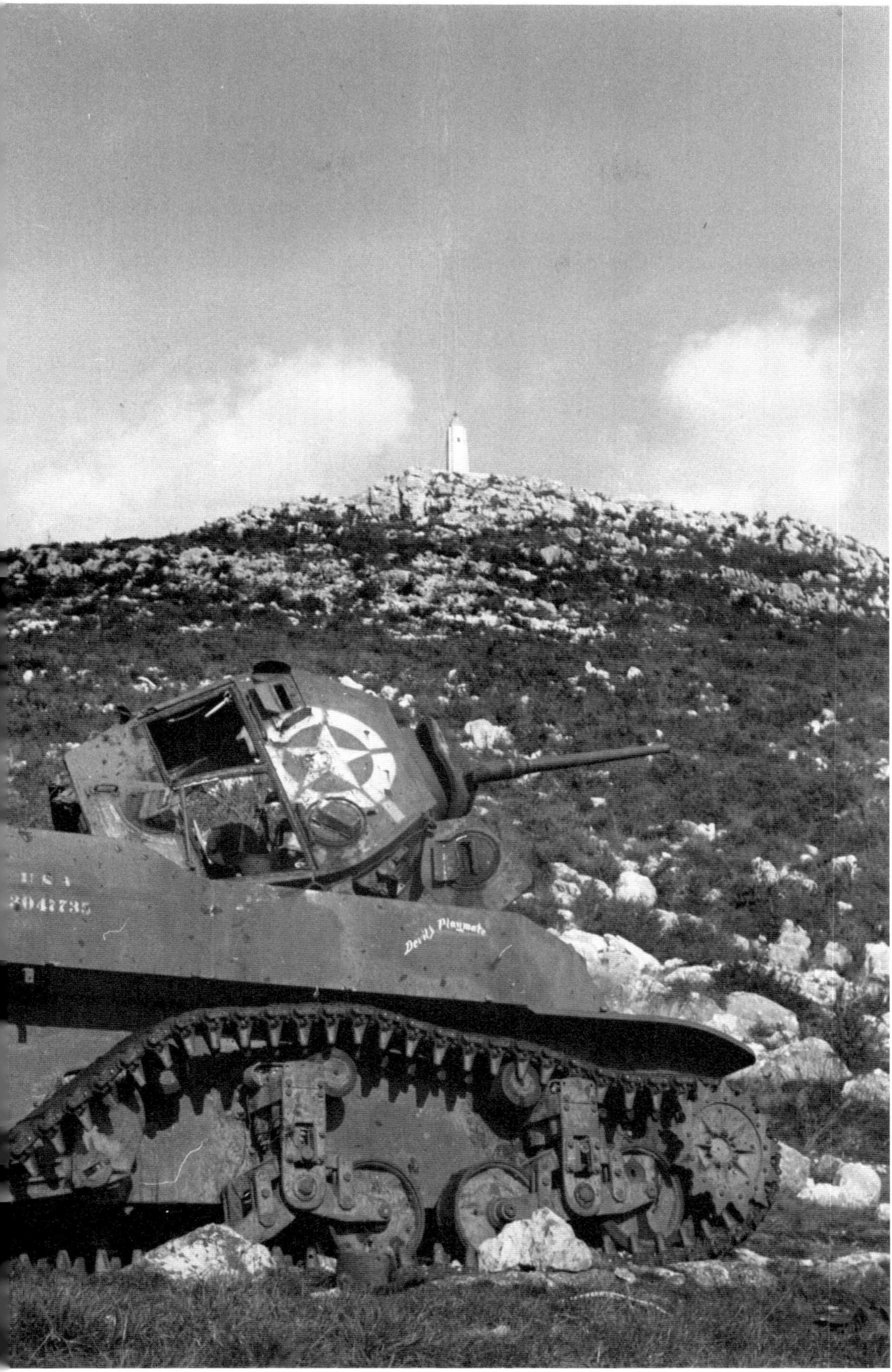
U S A
Devil's Playmate

Before they could get back for the gunner and me the Germans had taken us captive. The Germans separated us that night. They took me to a POW hospital as my foot was badly swollen from the mine explosion. Where they took the gunner, or what happened to him (I believe it was Wilbur Griffiths), I never found out.[42]

At the same time, efforts were made to evacuate Lieutenant Crews and his men. When one of the Indian recce tanks pulled alongside their disabled Stuart, Private John W. Sedicum volunteered to stay aboard and provide covering fire with the hull machine gun while Crews operated both guns in the turret.[43] The other crewmen in the tank transferred successfully but Crews and Sedicum had to hold out against the paratroopers for another 45 minutes until Private Arthur F. Lehman's tank arrived to take them off.

In the meantime Eckel returned to Custer's tank armed with more Teller mines fixed with igniters (allowing them to be used as satchel charges).[44] These he heaved into the turret. The resulting explosion destroyed the tank, ripping the turret off in the process.[45]

Further back, the Americans ran into problems with the poor terrain. Private Harold Hite's Stuart slipped over into a crater beside an old water

Private Harold Hite's tank stuck in soft ground near the water tank by Albaneta House. Two of his crew were rescued but Hite and one other man were left behind and reported missing in action. (*Polish Institute and Sikorski Museum*)

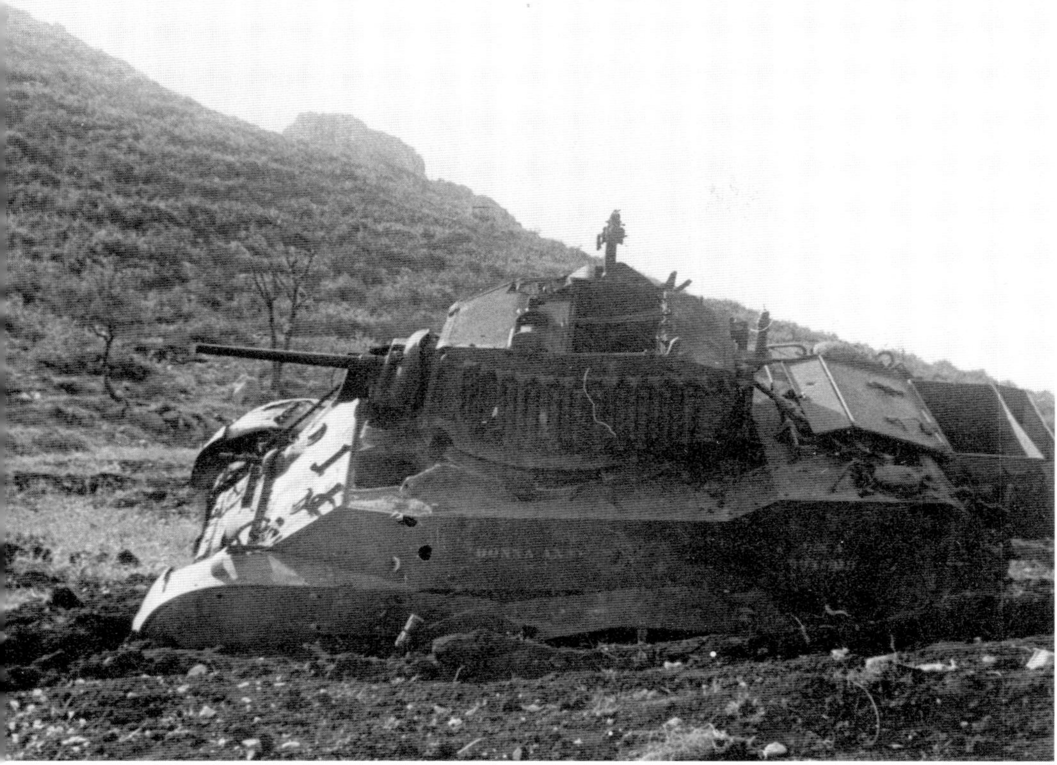

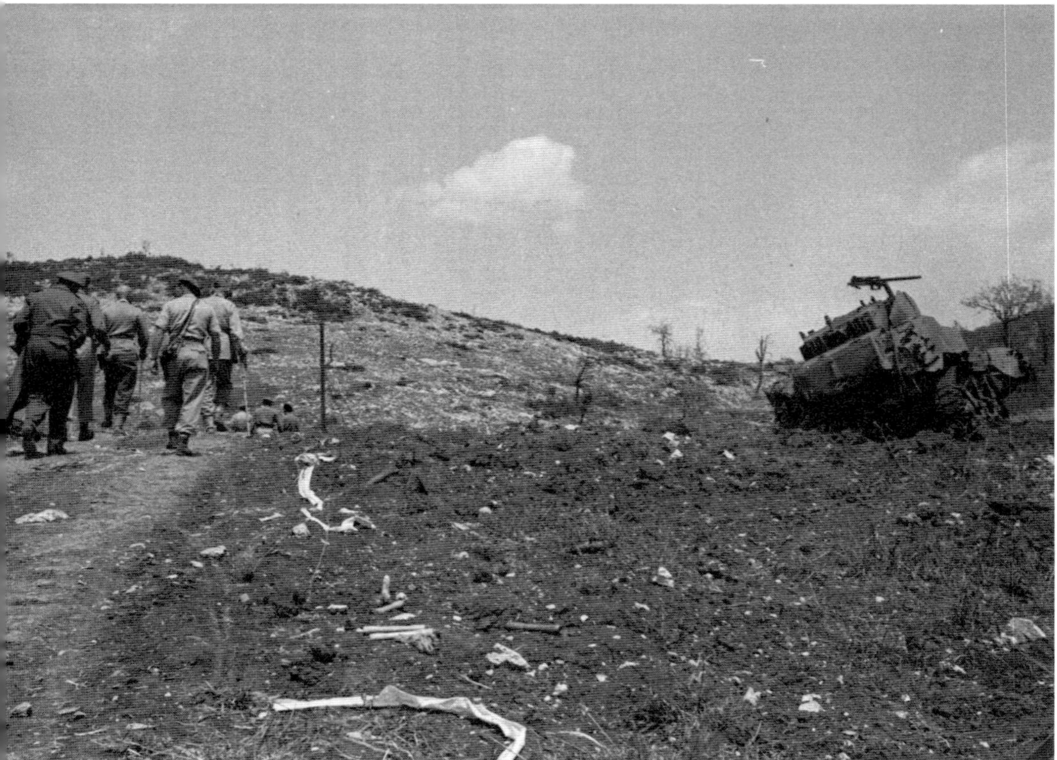

Sergeant Leonard E. Reese's tank also got stuck in the soft going. Two of the crew were in the process of being evacuated in Second Lieutenant Chester Wright's tank (most probably *Do or Die*) when it also became stuck. Wright and one of the men he had rescued from Reese's disabled tank were then rescued by Second Lieutenant James W. De Right in his tank. However, Technician Fifth Grade Selvidge, while attempting to aid the other man rescued from Reese's Stuart, was wounded by snipers, as was the man he was helping. Both were left behind. (*Polish Institute and Sikorski Museum*)

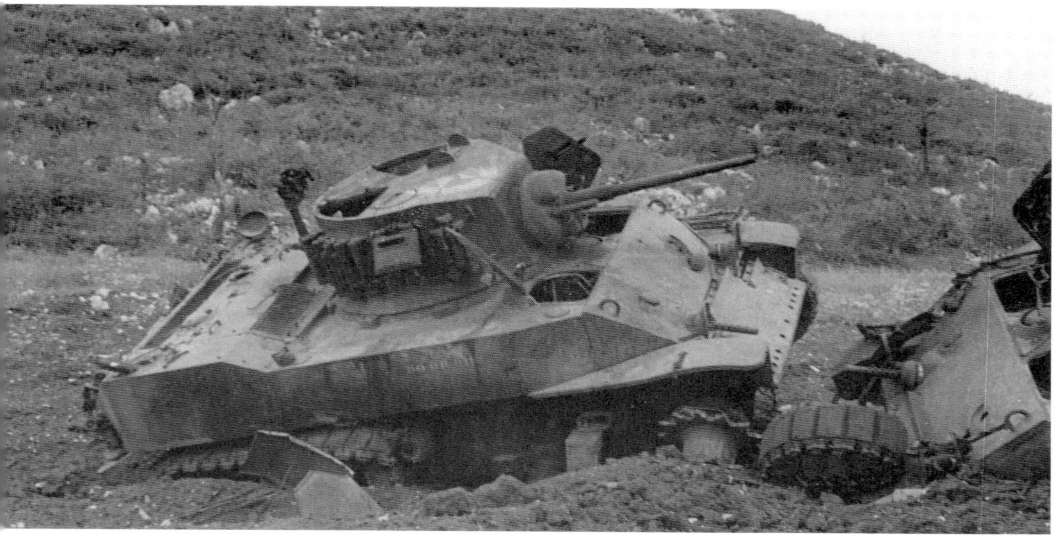

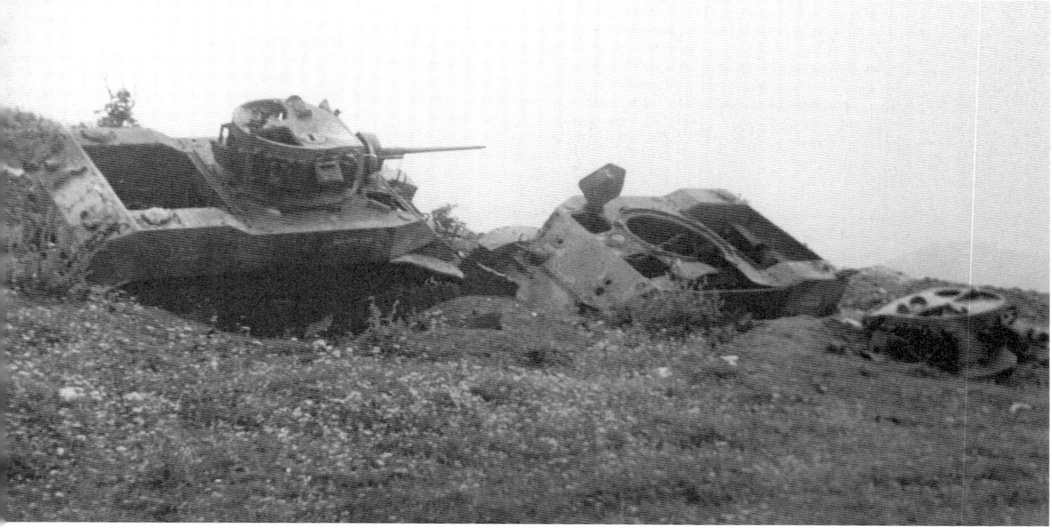

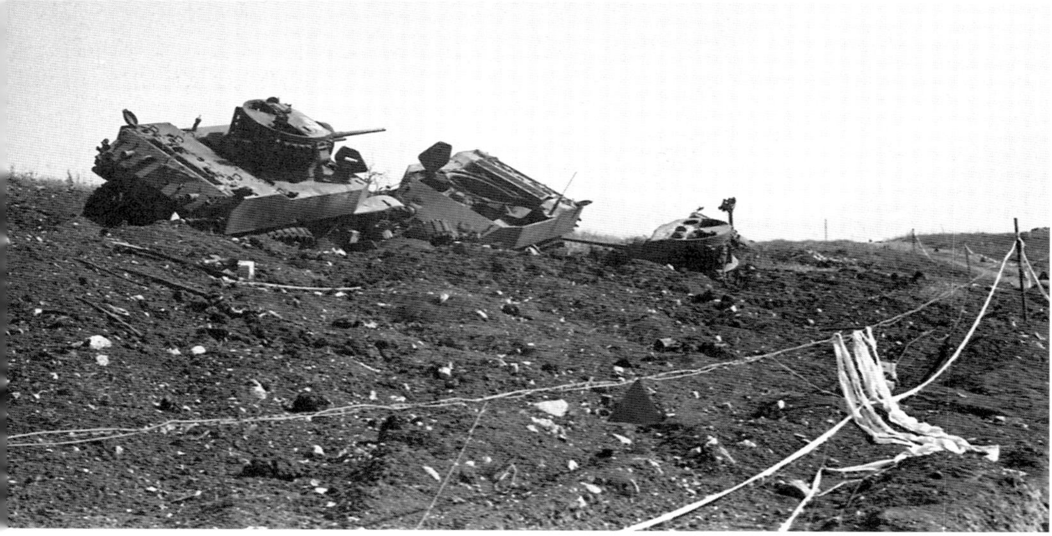

tank. Two of his crew managed to get out and, under covering fire, made their way back to the other tanks, where they were picked up by Lehman's tank. The other two crewmen, including Hite himself, remained with the tank and were later reported missing in action.

Back in the vicinity of Lennie's capsized Sherman, Sergeant Leonard E. Reese's Stuart became bogged in the soft ground, so 2nd Lieutenant Chester Wright came forward in his tank to attempt to rescue the three men from it.[46] He managed to get two men off, only to slip into a crater and become stuck himself. Wright and one other man were eventually pulled out by De Right in his tank but in the process Technician 5th Grade Richard H. Selvidge and the man he was trying to help into the tank were wounded by a sniper. De Right pulled back safely, leaving them behind, all further efforts to rescue them having to be abandoned.

The remaining tanks withdrew to the crest of the ridge overlooking Massa Albaneta. Except for some sniper fire and desultory shelling, the Germans held their fire. It was then that Barton was recalled to their start line, as Jim Moodie recalled:[47]

> I was on rear link, being Battle Captain, rear link back to the Brigadier. I pick up the switch and declare that we are at Point 593. There was no point in wireless security because Jerry could see that we were there. So you get it over quick and without any code, you had code where necessary. Told them where we were and asked for further instructions and [was told] in a very English voice 'Send Sunray [Barton] back here.'

As Barton later related:[48]

> Col. [Adye] asked me to go back for a conference with him – Captain Moodie was left in charge. Col. [Adye] asked me what I thought of the chances of getting to the monastery – I told him I thought they were 100-1 against and with only about five runners left and daylight fading fast it would be very rash to make any further attempt unless a diversion was urgently needed. I was strongly supported by Major Cruickshank of the Hussars. There appeared to be no infantry attack made such as we were expecting. Col. [Adye] then ordered us to return to the start line.

In the meantime Moodie ordered the surviving tanks to a position on the track north of Massa Albaneta where they were no longer visible to the German OPs; here they remained for the rest of the day, driving off with

After the battle this photograph was taken of Lennie's Sherman III and Reese's and Wright's M5A1s below the Bottleneck.

machine-gun fire some paratroopers who tried to stalk the tanks. Moodie also called up three or four of the Stuarts from Company D and sent them up to a crest above the track to harass the Germans to the west.

With light fading and all avenues of exploiting towards the monastery exhausted, there was nothing more they could do. Thus, at 5.30pm they were ordered to withdraw to their assembly area for the night. Moodie recalled that as they began to pull back, the German defenders gave them a departing gift:[49]

> We were there all day until five o'clock at night, it was coming slightly dusky and word came up on the phones, Pat Barton he said 'Return to Madras Circus.' As we started to go back the Jerries woke up then and all around us the scrub was just like a Guy Fawkes night, flashes and winkles of fire as they were shooting at us as they farewelled the tanks.

From this position, Lieutenant Crews again moved forward to the four Stuart tanks of his platoon that had been knocked out in the attempted attack upon Phantom House and removed the breechblocks from their 37mm guns. Thereafter the tank he was commanding threw a track, leaving behind another tank in the vicinity.

Chapter 12

Endgame

After pulling back to Madras Circus that night, the remnants of the force were subjected to another round of shelling, as Jim Moodie recalled:[1]

> It was night time and at night time you have to have one man up in the tank, alert ready for any assault on the tank itself. It was a brilliant night. So after the stress of the day we were all – to put it impolitely – buggered. So, [in] my tank, I took the first duty to let the boys sleep. By the time we got to Madras and had some tucker it was dark. That's what happened, here's me in the turret, no radio or anything like that on, listening and occasionally we'd get shelled and you're waiting for anything to be able to defend yourself against from the enemy, we're scattered. A shell landed alongside my tank. I got a smack up round the back.

Barton's driver, Trooper George Hanrahan, was badly wounded, as was his spare driver, Trooper Thomas Bell. Bell died in hospital six days later.

The Americans and Indians pulled out the following night, while C Squadron, 20 Armoured Regiment, all but withdrew on 22 March. One troop was left behind to support the Essex infantry, firstly under Jack Denham.

Miller and his crew remained in their tank at the bottom of the hill for some time too, according to Allan Coleman:[2]

> We sat there for some days and although an occasional shell passed close overhead, apparently Jerry could not hit us. Owing to the angle of the tank it was most uncomfortable. At one stage the driver found a bottle of rum behind the tank's instrument board and with our courage fortified we decided (driver and spare driver) that we would sleep that night in a cave further behind us. We had no sooner got out than an 88mm screeched by, just above our heads, and our courage and need for sleep evaporated.

Fortunately for all of those involved, the idea of renewing the attack the following day was abandoned; in any event, there were not enough tanks

The morning after the attack Captain Jim Moodie (his arm in a sling, injured by a piece of stray shrapnel) was photographed having breakfast with his crew. From left to right: Baird, Stillburn, 'Shorty' Shorrocks, Moodie, 'Digger' Grant. (*Jim Moodie*)

Shermans from C Squadron, 20 NZ Armoured Regiment, in Madras Circus after the failed attack up Cavendish Road. (*Jim Moodie*)

to carry on. After the tanks pulled out, the Germans made moves to close off the area to further armoured incursions. A group of paratroopers started laying mines on the track to the monastery and the surrounding land. They also set about destroying the tanks abandoned by Massa Albaneta and later on in the valley beyond the Bottleneck.

This did not stop at least one attempt to recover one of the tanks or the breechblock from it. Rex Miller and his crew had left their tank at the bottom of the hill to man one of the tanks in Madras Circus. Here Miller was called by the infantry with them to undertake a small job for them, as he later recalled:[3]

> One of the tanks coming back from the attack up the valley had thrown a track out in front of the Essex Regiment. They were concerned that the Germans might use the gun that was still mounted in the turret against them. An Essex officer came to us to see if we would go forward with a patrol to try to disable the gun. [Second Lieutenant] Laurie Falconer was the troop officer at the time and he called for somebody to go with them and I said I would. We had an Essex officer and sergeant and a section of about eight infantry. We went in single file till we got to the stage where you could see the silhouette of [the tank] in the dark. Then this jolly Spandau opened up from the side of the tank and got Laurie (he lost his right arm in the end) and he passed out there. When the Spandau opened up, we all scattered. The Tommies shot back and I shot back too. Then the sergeant said: 'Your mate's back there badly hurt.' So I went back to get him. I managed to half-drag him, half-carry him back quite some distance till I couldn't get any further. I went away and got my tank driver, Don Grant, with a stretcher, and we got Laurie back.

While Miller and the Essex troops were unable to disable the gun in the tank, some engineers from 4 NZ Armoured Brigade Recovery Section under Captain George Andrews were asked if they could recover some of the tanks at the top of the road. As Andrews later recalled:

> I took a team of boys to have a look around, they became rather thrilled at the thought of bringing these tanks down on a rocky surface where only four-wheel-drive vehicles could go and one slip could be [a] 200–300 feet fall. So that night we made special equipment so that we could use the tank brakes and the brakes on the two tractors and, without power from the tanks, guide them down the hill, one at a

time. This we successfully did; [it took] about an hour for each tank to come down over the 2.5-mile trip. The commander of the corps workshops was very pleased about this but that wasn't the opinion of Col. Uniacke when he saw me a few days later. We felt rather pleased about it though because every tank after we got it to the bottom was able to be started (though the batteries were flat) and driven away to the div.[4]

On 2 April the three tanks left at Madras Circus were handed over to a Canadian unit. Eventually they were pulled out and their places taken by British troops. They moved up a troop of M10 tank destroyers in response to fears that the Germans had deployed some tanks on the Cassino massif. The tanks ended up in the hands of Polish troops and were used by them in their operations in May.

Meanwhile, down on the plains below, things went from bad to worse for Freyberg. Parkinson was eventually forced to deploy the rest of 5 NZ Brigade in Cassino, not that it made any difference. Further efforts to clear the Hotel Continental corner of Route 6 came to naught. An attack by 21 NZ Battalion went in on the night of 20/21 March but made little headway. During the morning's fighting the battalion lost an entire platoon after the paratroopers in the hotel area launched a sortie under covering fire from the assault gun with them. The offensive finally ground to a halt on 23 March and the troops around Cassino went over to the defensive. Three days later the NZ Corps was dissolved and responsibility for the sector was handed over to the British XIII Corps.

* * *

Monte Cassino eventually fell to the Poles on 18 May 1944. Their attack on the mountain was part of a major offensive by the Allied forces in Italy. Known as Operation Diadem, this was launched on 11 May across the entire front from the sea to the mountains and involved the American Fifth Army, the *Corps Expéditionnaire Français* and the British Eighth Army. With Monte Cassino finally in Allied hands, and the route of their attack now cleared of enemy troops, those who took part in Operation Revenge finally had the opportunity to examine the ground they had fought over. On 29 May Len Gallagher made the following entry in his diary:

> Arrived back at 12.30. Bill de Lautour and Lou Hazlett had just come back. They had been up at Madras Circus and the Nunnery on top of the hill where we last went into action. They found Stuffy Hazlett's

Visiting the battlefield afterwards, Jim Moodie took this photograph of 'Stuffy' Hazlett's grave with Massa Albaneta in the background. Also visible are two of the abandoned M5A1s from the US attack, specifically Crews' tank in the foreground and Hite's tank further back. (*Jim Moodie*)

grave. He had been buried two days earlier by the Poles. They also found the bodies of Jack Dasler and George Sorich. They were still in the same shell hole as where they were last seen and were half buried. They buried them properly. Bill says a shell had landed on the edge of their hole. He says the shell hole was only 10 yards away from where we finished up in the tank in front of the Nunnery. I still cannot understand why, if they were still alive, they did not make a break for the tank when I started up the motors again. They must have heard them. Perhaps by then they had copped it as shit was landing all the time. I had hoped they had been [taken prisoner]. Now the doubt is eliminated, one can only say three fine chaps gone in the whole cost of war's sadism.[5]

Gallagher had the opportunity to visit the site when the division was at rest in the area around Arce. On July he made the following entry in his diary:

We went up what is called the Tornado track to Madras Circus, where we took our tanks in the attack on the Nunnery. I consider it a tribute to our drivers that all but one tank reached the top. The road is only just wide enough to take a tank, very steep and sharp corners. The Poles attacked the monastery via this road and two of their tanks went over the bank and are still lying there. Bill Craig's tank had been blown up by Jerry and also George Healy's turret's blown right off. In the first basin were four Honeys burned out. A little further on was a mass Polish grave. Then we came to the Nunnery. There was another mass Polish grave. I saw Stuffy Hazlett's grave, also where Jack and George are buried. The area is heavily mined and there are bazooka bombs, grenades and other debris of war lying everywhere. From

This was where the tank force was aiming for: the track down to the monastery. Of note here is the absolute devastation that Len Gallagher later wrote about in his diary. (*Brendon O'Carroll*)

here a cobbled path leads to the monastery. This is as far as we reached with our tank attack, and were to go along it to the monastery, but there was no sign of our infantry and we had to pull out. Jeff Townsend's tank was still in the same place, Jerry had burned it up. Nearby were three Yank Honeys demolished, and the graves of some of the crews. We walked along the cobbled path, and I do not think it was possible to get a Sherman along it. In any case Jerry had only to stop the first tank and that would block the rest. The monastery was a walk of about half a mile. The place was devastated. All the trees were stripped bare and cut to pieces and there was not a patch of earth that had not been churned up. Bomb craters were much in evidence. The whole terrain was a formidable defence position. The monastery itself is completely wrecked above ground and it was built of solid stone with much marble interior finish. It is a huge building covering to my estimate about 5 acres. There will be a colossal amount of work involved if they ever rebuild it. The motor road to the monastery from Cassino is completely wrecked. The view is wonderful. Jerry could see every movement in daylight and it is strange that he did not shell us more than he did.[6]

Chapter 13

The Attack in Retrospect

It probably goes without saying that there was much disappointment within Revenge Force over the failure of the attack. Those who took part had also lost many good comrades for no apparent gain. Casualties in the New Zealand squadron amounted to five killed and six wounded, one man from the Indian squadron was wounded, and the Americans had five men killed, nine wounded and three taken prisoner: a total of twenty-nine men from the whole force. Losses in tanks had been high, too. Of the C Squadron tanks, three were left behind as unrecoverable, three were damaged but driven out, and another three were ditched but recoverable. Losses among the other units consisted of one of the Indian Shermans, two of their Stuart Recce tanks and ten American light tanks. In total, losses amounted to nineteen tanks out of the forty-four sent into the action.

When it comes to the Third Battle of Cassino, the Cavendish Road attack has been overlooked by most authors. This is despite the fact that immediately after the attack it was presented to the general public, including in New Zealand, as a success, this report in the *Otago Daily Times* for 20 March 1944 being typical:

> Allied tanks are rolling over a secretly built mountain road and have outflanked the German positions at Cassino, says a British United Press correspondent. The tank forces, after seizing Mount [sic] Albaneta, are now approaching the road to Rome.

Afterwards, Freyberg, somewhat dismissively, wrote in his report to the New Zealand government that:[1]

> It appeared in the morning, however, that though delayed, the attack on the monastery from Point 435 would go in and the hook of the armour via Cavendish Road was not stopped. From intercepts it was clear that the appearance of tanks on the enemy left was a complete surprise and caused the enemy considerable anxiety. One intercept was that the tanks had broken through the enemy's main line of

resistance. This attack, however, was no more than a diversion and was finally held by mines and the going, and the [tanks] withdrew to our FDLs before dark. They were not accompanied by infantry. Had they been, the infantry would have been pinned to the ground by enemy [small arms] fire from a strong enemy position.

Perhaps this is why the Cavendish Road attack has been relegated to the background in most accounts.

Of all the attempts to break the deadlock at Cassino, the Cavendish Road attack comes over as perhaps one of the most inspired operations. The idea of sending a tank force up the mountains behind the monastery was worthy of German tactical thinking; the pity was that it was so badly mishandled in the end. But it should not have been like that. One thing apparent from the operational orders was that there were strict guidelines as to when it could be launched. It is also apparent that these were closely adhered to until the day before its launch. This is because the operation was simply meant to be a reconnaissance-in-force. At the bare minimum it was simply to test the German lines after the breakout into the Liri valley and the fall of the monastery. The most optimistic outcome would be to spread mayhem and despair behind enemy lines. While there were no strict timelines for the attack on the monastery by the Indians, had things gone according to plan then the Indians would probably have launched their attack up the eastern slopes of the Cassino massif around dusk, as that was when 6 NZ Brigade was expected to be on the second objective, Phaseline Jockey. Exactly when the Indians were to launch their attack on the monastery itself was never specified but the expectation was that it would have been sometime on 16 March, possibly as late as dawn. Had it happened then, with the Germans bound to launch a counter-attack to retake it, the appearance of a tank force behind Snakeshead Ridge, with or without infantry, could have thrown any such enemy efforts into disarray.

To have launched Revenge alone, without the other arm (the Gurkha attack on the monastery from Hangman's Hill), and without their own infantry support, was asking too much. The German paratroopers against whom the attack fell were no strangers to dealing with tanks unsupported by infantry. The question remains, would the inclusion of infantry in the attack have made any difference? Infantry would certainly have enabled the tank force to deal with any of the German paratroopers who came forward to surrender, and maybe even helped the tanks to secure Massa Albaneta. They would, however, have been very vulnerable to fire from the German defenders from both Point 593 and Phantom Ridge, as the Poles discovered in May. In fact, without some means of diverting the attention of the Germans on the heights above the valley, it is doubtful if infantry support would have worked. This fact alone points to the interrelatedness of the defences here, a fact later recognised by the Poles and succinctly expressed by them in their combat report:

> Enemy posns covered MASSA ALBANETA, hills 593, 569, PHANTOM R, high ground S ANGELO, hills 575, 505, 433 and 447 forming, as it were, a ring around all these hills and ridges. The valley in-between was NOT actually occupied by the enemy. This def[ensive] lay-out enabled the enemy to fire down from all strongpoints sited around this ring to bear on any of the def sector. At the same time any of our attacking tps, on breeching enemy defs in a narrow sector, would come under enfilade fire from many directions, and it would be only by capturing at least half of these ring defs, i.e. at least hill 593, PHANTOM RIDGE and S ANGELO, that any such enfilade fire would be rendered out of the question. This would allow the holding of captured objectives and by this very fact the creating of favourable conditions for a further attack.[2]

Based on this assessment, the Poles reached the conclusion that simply attacking the ring at a single point was unlikely to succeed. Thus, a single thrust like that of Operation Revenge was likely to fail unless conducted simultaneously with attacks on Point 593 and Phantom Ridge. This is what the Americans found out in February when they attacked Point 593 and Colle Sant'Angelo at the same time. So long as both positions were under attack, the Germans were forced to divide their fire between the two attacking forces. When the American attack on Colle Sant'Angelo failed, the Germans were then able to focus all their fire on the attack on Point 593. Fortunately by this stage the Americans had secured Point 593.

Ultimately the Americans lost control of Point 593 when a small group of German paratroopers overcame them in a surprise attack. With that went their chance to unhinge the Gustav Line as well. In the end they did not realise just how close they had been to success there. Generalleutnant Fridolin von Senger und Etterlin later admitted that he had seriously considered withdrawing from Monte Cassino if the Americans had been successful in taking Colle Sant'Angelo. Why? Because with those strategic positions in their hands, the Americans would have been able to direct counter-battery fire onto his own artillery in the Liri valley, thus depriving the Germans of their much-needed fire support. Whether of course the paratroopers would have given up their hold on Monte Cassino is another matter; they certainly were very reluctant to do so in May 1944 and had to be ordered off by the commander of the German armies in Italy, Kesselring.

Even if Freyberg or Galloway been aware of this when planning the attack by 4 Indian Division, there was probably little they could have done about it. The units from 7 Indian Brigade had suffered heavily in their attempts to take Point 593 in February and were in no position to renew their assault in that direction. Nor were the other two brigades in any position to assist: 5 Indian Brigade had been committed to the assault on the monastery via Hangman's Hill and 11 Indian Brigade had been relegated to a support role. For Freyberg to have diverted one of his units intended for the breakout phase into what was supposed to be just a reconnaissance-in-force would have been seen by him as a further dilution of his main effort. Certainly 22 NZ Motor Battalion could have been made available to support the tanks but only at the expense of his exploitation force and he would still not have had enough troops for the attack along the Snakeshead and Phantom Ridge axes. In the end the Cavendish Road attack did not alter the course of the battle one iota. The tanks were driven back by a determined enemy who was not at all fazed by their appearance.

This does raise the question as to why the attack was allowed to go ahead in the first place. Throughout the early stages of the battle the Indians had been reluctant even to attack the monastery, thanks to the vulnerable position in which the Gurkhas had ended up. By 18 March they were adamant that it would not go ahead until New Zealand troops had cleared the town but it was looking like that was not going to happen fast. And then it all suddenly changed within the space of a few hours. What brought about this change? Did the attack by a lone German aircraft on a column of American tanks on Cavendish Road trigger the whole operation? Certainly this could have been the factor that convinced Galloway to launch 5 Indian Brigade against the monastery. But when this failed, the tank attack could still have been called off. By that stage, however, the tanks were already in Madras Circus and the chance of them being discovered by the Germans was high. Perhaps Freyberg thought there was no other choice but to go on.

PART III

ON THE TRAIL OF REVENGE TODAY

Chapter 14

A Visitor's Guide to Cavendish Road

Via Orsaia-Fonnone to Cavendish Road

Travelling north from Cassino, the road to Caira village (Via Caira) passes the sites of the former Italian barracks, remnants of which can still be seen as either intact buildings or the foundations of others. Beyond this the road crosses a dried-up channelled watercourse, next to which, and running up to the left, is a narrow paved road, the Via Chaia. Following this road will lead to a cluster of houses, Lazio, which was the site of the Indian regimental aid post (**A**). Beyond Lazio the road becomes the Via Fonnone, which shortly afterwards meets the Via Cavatelle on the right from Caira

The lower stretch of Cavendish Road. (*Google Earth*)

(**A**) The Indian regimental aid post was located in the hamlet of Lazio, where the Via Chaia becomes the Via Cavatelle. (*Perry Rowe*)

A Visitor's Guide to Cavendish Road 135

and the Via Monacato to the left. Approximately 120 metres along the Via Monacato, a rough farm track marks the start of Cavendish Road, these days marked by both a signpost and an information board.

Caira Village to Cavendish Road

The alternative way to access Cavendish Road is from the town of Caira, where the various elements of Revenge Force assembled before the attack. Caira is located 4km north of Cassino and is reached by way of the Via Caira, which turns into the Corso San Basilio once inside the village. This was one of the original routes used by New Zealand troops to enter Cassino on 15 March 1944. Access to Cavendish Road can be obtained by following the Via Cavatelle, which leads off from a roundabout on the Corso San Basilio. Corporal Miller's tank slipped off the road part way along the Via Cavatelle (**B**), within sight of present-day Caira.

Following the Via Cavatelle will bring visitors to the junction with the Via Fonnone, which descends through Lazio to the Rapido valley, joining up with the Via Caira just to the north of the 1944 Italian barracks. The Via Monacato to the right leads up to the start of Cavendish Road (**C**),

Access to Cavendish Road can be had from the Corso San Basilio in the village of Caira, from where the Via Cavatelle leads up to the Via Fonnone and the Via Monacato. (*Pino Valente*)

(**B**) Corporal Rex Miller's tank ran off the Via Cavatelle near here on its way up the junction with the Via Fonnone and the Via Monacato. (*Perry Rowe*)

(**C**) Looking for all the world like a rough farm track, the entrance to Cavendish Road lies on the Via Monacato approximately 125m past the junction with the Via Fonnone and the Via Cavatelle. The signpost and information board are recent additions. (*Pino Valente*)

approximately 125m beyond the junction. At this point Cavendish Road resembles nothing more than a rutted farm track, only the recently erected signpost and an information noticeboard revealing its historical significance.

Cavendish Road to Madras Circus

Cavendish Road then climbs gently up an avenue of trees from the entrance, turning from a farm track into more of a formed road (**D**). From there it starts to swing around the side of Monte Castellone (**E**) and provides the first view of the road beyond the first nullah or dry watercourse (**F**) (see p. 27). Some of the stonework is evident around the first tight corner of the road at the first of the nullahs (**G**). The road then swings around a small spur (**H**) towards the second nullah. It was in this area, relatively safe from observation from the Germans, that ammunition and other supplies were stored (see p. 29).

The upper portion of Cavendish Road across the nullahs to Madras Circus. (*Google Earth*)

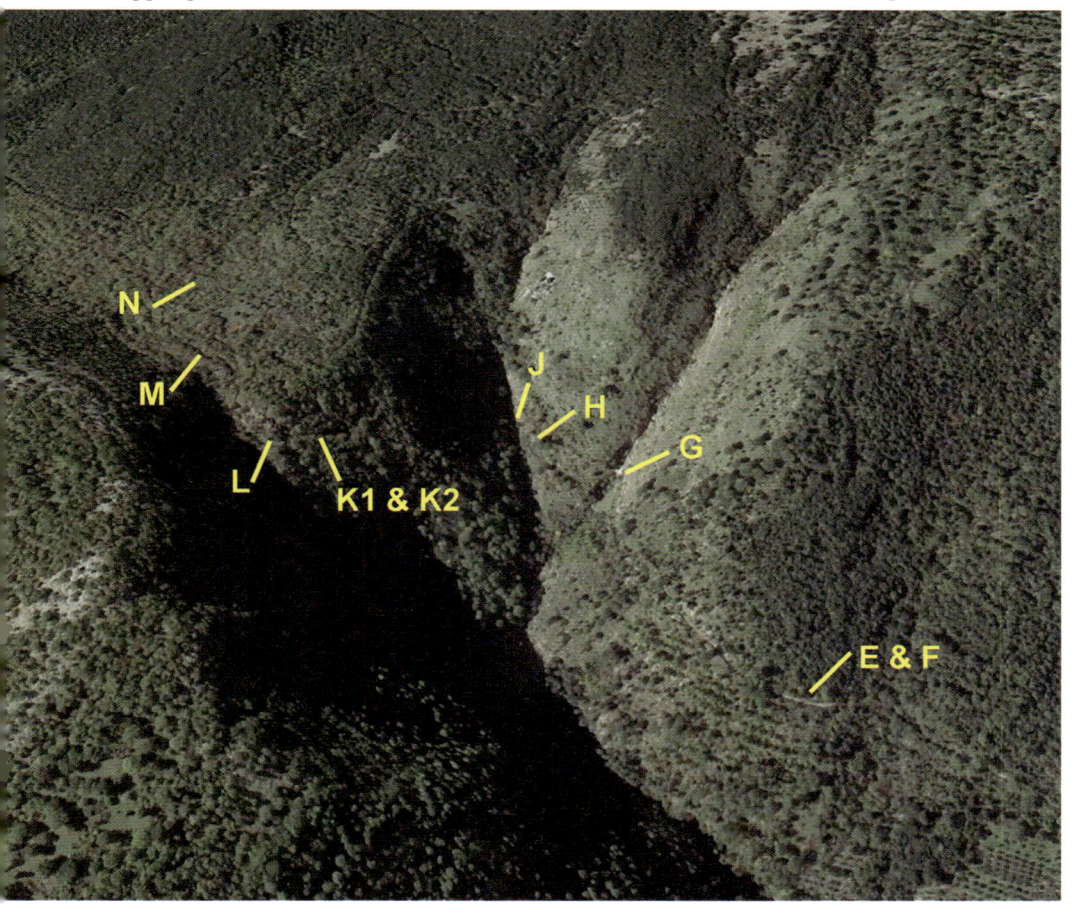

(**D**) Beyond the entrance the cart track gives way to a short paved stretch of road. (*Perry Rowe*)

(**E**) At the first bend on the road … (**F**) the upper reaches of the road up towards Madras Circus become visible. (*Perry Rowe*)

(**G**) Some of the stonework at the bend of the first nullah is still evident. (*Perry Rowe*)

The second nullah (**J**) is much overgrown today, though part of the bluff face is still exposed (see p. 30). The road then proceeds through some areas of thick bush and scrub before emerging in a clear area that provides a good view of the road leading up to the first nullah (**K1** & **K2**) (see p. 34). Traces of the lower mule track can still be made out through the treeline. The road then swings around a sharp bend into a small gully that leads up towards Madras Circus (**L**) (see p. 36). Now heavily overgrown with trees, this is where the US tanks were parked up for three days before the attack was launched. At this point, just before Cavendish Road reaches Madras Circus, Colle Maiola comes into view (**M**). The open meadow of Madras Circus has largely been overtaken by bush and scrub but a few years ago the area where C Squadron, 20 NZ Armoured Regiment, parked their tanks following the attack was still relatively clear (see p. 120).

These days it is not possible to get from Madras Circus to the valley between Snakeshead and Phantom Ridges (**N**). Instead a track, the Via Santa Maria dell'Albaneta, leads off after the second nullah and proceeds through the bush and trees, entering the valley just before the first

A Visitor's Guide to Cavendish Road 141

(**H**) A lot of mortar ammunition was discarded along the section of the road between the nullahs. (*Perry Rowe*)

(J) The second nullah. (*Perry Rowe*)

(**K1** & **K2**) From this point a good view can be had of the road running up to the first nullah. (*Perry Rowe*)

(L) Round the final bend up to Madras Circus the road enters a narrow valley where the US tanks were hidden under camouflage netting on the days leading up to the attack. (*Perry Rowe*)

(**M**) Just before Cavendish Road enters Madras Circus, the shoulder of Point 603 becomes visible. (*Perry Rowe*)

(**N**) Today Madras Circus, where the New Zealand tanks laagered after the attack, is heavily overgrown with bush and scrub and it is not possible to get into the valley before the first bottleneck from here. (*Perry Rowe*)

constriction in the valley. For those not wishing to walk up Cavendish Road, access can be gained to Massa Albaneta and the valleys beyond from the Polish Cemetery car park on Monte Cassino.

Madras Circus to Massa Albaneta

Just beyond Madras Circus the scrub and trees open out to a flat, grassy valley between Point 706 and Colle Maiola, where Owen Hughes', Jock Laidlaw's and Jack Hazlett's tanks were abandoned. The ditch that Hazlett's tank slipped into is still there, marked by a line of scrub and bushes (**I**) (see p. 92). The track then passes through the first constriction (**II**), sometimes referred to as a bottleneck, and for this reason there is some confusion in accounts of the battle as to which bottleneck is being referred to. Beyond this constriction, the track enters another open area of grassland between Phantom Ridge and Snakeshead Ridge. Over to the north side of this valley is the area where the Stuarts from Company D became stuck in soft going while attacking Phantom Ridge (**III**) (see p. 91), though the area is now heavily overgrown with bush and scrub. Above

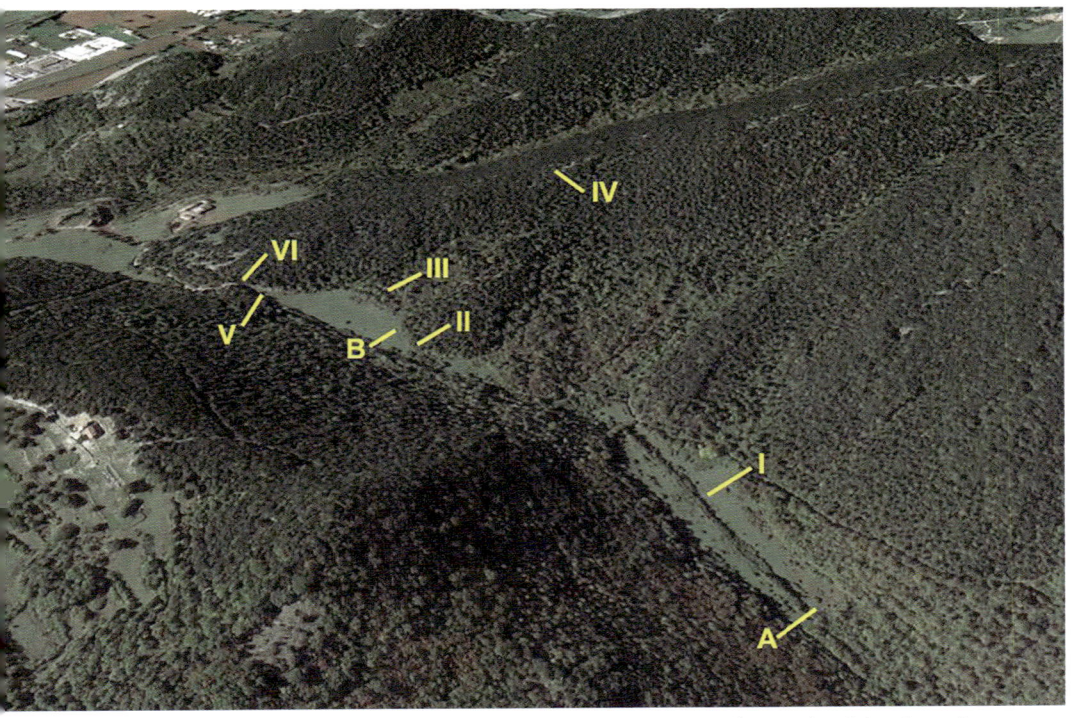

The valley between Snakeshead Ridge on the left and Phantom Ridge on the right. **A** marks the point where Owen Hugh's tank threw a track; **B** marks the point where Bill de Lautour's tank ran off its track. (*Google Earth*)

(**I**) The ditch where Lieutenant Jack Hazlett's tank capsized is still evident today, though now blocked with scrub and small trees. From here a gravel track enters the valley from the forest. (*Perry Rowe*)

(**II**) The gravel track on passing through the first bottleneck enters the second valley, where some more tanks were lost. (*Perry Rowe*)

(**III**) This was where a number of US tanks became mired in the soft ground below Phantom Ridge. (*Perry Rowe*)

(**IV**) The remains of Phantom House can still be found on the ridge above. (*Perry Rowe*)

the point where the US tanks became stuck can be found the remains of Phantom House (**IV**) (see p. 90). The track continues up towards the next bottleneck, at the foot of which is the Polish-crewed Sherman (**V**) that was destroyed by a double or triple Teller mine on 11 May, killing all its crew: the only true relic of the battle. The Poles left it as they found it when they turned it into a memorial.

The road then rises from the Polish memorial to the top of the 'Bottleneck' (**VI**) before descending to the flat grassy meadow around Massa Albaneta. The upper track used by the tanks to get past Massa Albaneta has largely disappeared under bush and scrub, leaving only the lower access road that passes close by Massa Albaneta, itself almost covered by trees and other vegetation. Reg Lennie's tank slipped into a crater on the Phantom Ridge side of the road, the car marking its approximate position (**VII**) (see p. 99). Reese's and De Wright's tanks came to grief on the opposite side of the track leading up to the 'Bottleneck' from Massa Albaneta (**VIII**) (see p. 117).

(**V**) The only original relic of the fighting is this Sherman III from the Polish 4 Armoured Regiment 'Skorpion', destroyed after running over a mine on 13 May, the explosion killing all its crew. After the battle the Poles turned it into this memorial. (*Jeffrey Plowman*)

The flat below Points 593 and 569 by Massa Albaneta where most of the fighting took place. '**A**' indicates where Private Harold Hite's tank was abandoned; '**B**' marks where Sergeant Leonard Reese's and Second Lieutenant Chester Wright's tanks were lost. (*Google Earth*)

(**VI**) These days the view of Massa Albaneta from the top of the Bottleneck is obscured by the new growth in trees. (*Jeffrey Plowman*)

(**VII**) The car marks the spot where Corporal Reg Lennie's tank capsized. Trees cover Massa Albaneta behind it. (*Perry Rowe*)

(**VIII**) Looking back from Massa Albaneta, this is the view the Germans would have had of the Bottleneck. (*Jeffrey Plowman*)

(**IX**) This is the view the Germans on Point 593 would have had of the fighting around Massa Albaneta. (*Perry Rowe*)

Bob Frettlohr outside Massa Albaneta. (*Bob Frettlohr*)

Massa Albaneta (earlier known as Masseria Albaneta) originally started out as a small monastery that the Benedictine monk San Lucido (960–1038) named Santa Maria dell'Albaneta. Later it became an overflow seminary from the main monastery. Masseria is the Sicilian and southern Italian word for farmhouse, which probably explains why it was often referred to in Allied accounts as Albaneta Farm. Massa Albaneta as seen from Point 593 (**IX**) shows what a commanding view its German occupiers had of the whole area from the open meadow in front of Massa Albaneta,

Jim Moodie and Karl Newedal (*left*) during the 50th Anniversary Commemoration at Cassino in 1994. Karl would later visit Jim in New Zealand. (*Jim Moodie*)

(**X**) This is the approximate place where Second Lieutenant John Crew's tank was knocked out; Monte Caira is in the background. (*Jeffrey Plowman*)

(**XI**) Sergeant Lawrence Custer's tank was destroyed in this grove of trees beyond Massa Albaneta. (*Jeffrey Plowman*)

A Visitor's Guide to Cavendish Road 155

(**XII**) Further down the track towards the monastery, Point 569 can be seen towering over the track, showing, like Point 593, what a commanding view its German defenders had of the attack. (*Perry Rowe*)

(**XIII**) This cave near the junction with the track up to Point 593 and the road down to the Polish Cemetery car park was the location of the headquarters of II Bataillon Fallschirmjäger-Regiment 4. (*Perry Rowe*)

including the area where the tanks were operating, to the twin peaks of Colle Sant'Angelo to the rear.

Crew's tank was lost just off the track to the monastery around this point (**X**) (see p. 107). Custer's tank was disabled just beyond there in a grove of trees (**XI**) (see p. 109). Walking further down the track to the monastery gives a view of Point 569 (**XII**), where Custer's tank was knocked out not more than 100m from the cave that served as the headquarters of II Bataillon Fallschirmjäger-Regiment 4 (**XIII**). Whatever the case, it may well have been the cave to which Eckel went to obtain the mines used against Custer's tank. Past the turn-off to Point 593 (now known as Monte Calvario) and the main Polish memorial, the road descends through a line of trees to the monastery.

APPENDICES

Appendix 1

Operational Orders

                                                  SECRET
                                                  Copy No.
                                                  21 Feb 44

<u>NZ CORPS OPERATION INSTRUCTION NO. 5</u>
Ref Map: 1/25,000 Sheets 160 I SW, 160 I SE, 160 II NW, 160 II NE.
<u>CONFIRMING VERBAL INSTRUCTIONS</u>
<u>INFM</u>
  1. <u>Enemy</u>
     As per NZ Corps Intelligence Summaries.
  2. <u>Own Tps</u>
     Present dispositions of tps within FIFTH ARMY remains unchanged and pressure is being exerted along the whole front.
  3. <u>Groupings</u>
     Groupings within NZ Corps remain unchanged.
<u>INTENTION</u>
  4. NZ Corps will attack and capture CASSINO exploiting so as to est bridgehead over R RAPIDO.
<u>METHOD</u>
  5. The op will be carried out in three phases:-
     Phase I – Preliminary ops prior to an attack on CASSINO
     Phase II – Air bombardment of CASSINO
     Phase III – Attack on CASSINO
<u>PHASE I</u>
  6. <u>Tasks</u>
     Following will be completed by first light 24 Feb:-
     (a) 2 NZ Div will
         (i) Relieve 91 US Recce Bn
        (ii) Relieve 133 US Inf Regt
       (iii) Posn all tps 2 NZ Div for the attack on CASSINO and deploy so as to bring maximum fire on enemy posns from East bank R RAPIDO.

(b) 4 Ind Div will
- (i) Attack and capture Pt 445 G845212
- (ii) Recce and constr posns on spurs along gen line Pt 450 G840214 – Pt 445 G853216 sited to cover by fire: Western outskirts of CASSINO and Eastern slopes of MONASTERY HILL.

PHASE II

7. D Day for Phase II will NOT be prior to 24 Feb and will be decided by the Air Comd. It will be promulgated on the previous night by the codeword 'BRADMAN' followed by the date.
8. Phase II consists of an air attack on CASSINO by approx
   12 Groups hy bombers
   7 Groups med bombers.
   Details of the air plan will be based on the requirements of 2 NZ Div and will be arranged by NZ Corps.
9. By first light on D Day all tps will be withdrawn outside the bomb safety line. Map refs defining the bomb safety line will be issued later.

PHASE III

10. Tasks
    (a) 2 NZ Div will attack and capture CASSINO and Pt. 193.
    (b) 4 Ind Div will
    - (i) From posns already constr assist with fire the attack of 2 NZ Div by neutralising enemy posns on the Eastern slopes MONTE CASSINO.
    - (ii) Take over Pt 193 G853213 after its capture by 2 NZ Div.
11. Zero Hr
    Will be immediately following Phase II and will be the time when the arty programme opens and inf adv for the attack on CASSINO commences. Exact hr will be notified later. NO bombs will be dropped on CASSINO after zero hr.
12. Bdys
    (a) 4 Ind Div right with 36 US Div – unchanged.
    (b) 2 NZ Div right with 4 Ind Div – all incl 2 NZ Div Pt 175 G853218 – Pt 193 G853213.
    (c) 2 NZ Div left with 10 Corps – unchanged.
13. Exploitation
    Exploitation will be carried out as follows:-
    (a) 2 NZ Div
       (i) To South to open up Highway 6.

  (ii) To East and SE to clear enemy between RAPIDO and GARI rivers so that constr of crossings over R RAPIDO can be effected.
 (b) <u>4 Ind Div</u>
  (i) Along Eastern slopes MONTE CASSINO to protect right flank 2 NZ Div.
  (ii) Vicinity Pt 193 G853213 to mop up enemy posts.
14. <u>Arty</u>
 (a) An active CB and HF policy will be adopted during Phases I and II.
 (b) Maximum arty support to be given during Phase III.
15. <u>Engrs</u>
 (a) Maint of fwd routes.
 (b) All available assistance to 2 NZ Div during Phase III.
 (c) Bridging of R RAPIDO as early as operational situation allows.

<u>ADM</u>
16. <u>Traffic</u>
 FMNs are responsible for lighting of routes and TC within their own areas.

<u>INTERCOMN</u>
17. HQ NZ Corps remains present location.
18. Codeword for op – 'DICKENS'.
19. ACK

            R.C. Queree
            Brigadier
            BGS, New Zealand Corps.
            Time of Signature 2300 hrs.

       *   *   *

Rear 4 Ind Div   Main 4 Ind Div,
CIEME (Rear Div pass)   11 Mar 44.
Main NZ Corps
1. D Coy, 760 US Tank Bn, comprising 17 STUART tanks, and subject to confirmation, one Pl of three SP 105mm guns, come under comd 7 Bde Recce Sqn forthwith and are concentrating in area 904217 by first light 12 Mar.
2. 7 Bde will be prepared to exploit the success of operation 'DICKENS' by directing 7 Bde Recce Sqn on axis CAVENDISH road–ALBANET house 832216 to area ALBANET house to disrupt

enemy in that area on slopes of Pt 593 feature 835215 and to exploit SOUTH EAST towards MONTE CASSINO 845208.
3. Timing
7 Bde Recce Sqn will move fwd from area 904217 via MICHELE and CAIRO roads on night D/D plus one, and lie up between CAIRO and MADRAS CIRCUS 839231 to debouch from MADRAS CIRCUS at first light D plus one day under orders from 7 Bde.
4. The code name for this operation will be REVENGE and zero hr will be the time 7 Bde Recce Sqn debouch from MADRAS CIRCUS.
5. APM will arrange Traffic Control in conjunction with 3 DIA to pass 7 Bde Recce Sqn against normal traffic circuit on CAIRO road between 2200 hrs and 2359 hrs on D Day. Thereafter the normal traffic circuit to CAIRO via VILLA road and CEMETERY road and from CAIRO via CAIRO road will be enforced.
6. RA
31 Fd Regt are in close support 7 Bde and will provide necessary FOOS for operation REVENGE both on ground within our present FDLs and on tanks to be provided by 7 Bde Recce Sqn.
7. RE
12 Fd Coy with one D-7 tractor and two D-4 bulldozers under comd is in close support 7 Bde and will provide RE task force as required by comd 7 Bde.
CRE will arrange for the D-7 tractor to be in MADRAS CIRCUS area by last light D Day for towing and recovery purposes and for the two D-4 bulldozers to be CAIRO area by last light D Day and that comd 7 Bde considers it is reasonably safe for them to do so.
8. Bulldozers, D-7 tractor, soft skinned vehs and personnel will not move fwd of MADRAS CIRCUS until the situation is such that comd Bde considers it reasonably safe for them to do so.
9. Sigs.
7 Bde Recce Sqn is on 7 Bde fwd control net. 7 Bde Recce Sqn will arrange wireless comn with D Coy 760 US Tank Bn and the SP 105mm Pl under mutual arrangements.
10. D Day is the day on which operation DICKENS commences.
11. Rptd 3 DIA.
Request your fwd tps on CASTELLONE feature be instructed to take advantage of any situation this operation may create by exploiting down CASTELLONE SPUR and to give any assistance

they can by fire under mutual arrangements to be made direct with comd 7 Ind. Inf Bde.

* * *

7 IND. INF. BDE. OPERATIONAL ORDER NO. 33.   15 Mar 44.

Refer maps:-
  1/50,000 sheets 160 (I, II, III and IV).
  1/25,000 sheets 160 I SW.
                  160 II SE.
                  160 III NE.
                  160 IV NW.

INTRODUCTION
1. <u>ENEMY</u> no change. 1 Para. Div. is believed to be holding from Mt. CASTELLONE to include CASSINO town.
2. <u>OWN TROOPS</u>
   (a) <u>NZ Corps</u> is to carry out Operation DICKENS to break through and destroy the enemy in the CASSINO sector. 'D' Day 15 Mar '44.
   (b) <u>Air Bombardment</u>
       The operation is to begin with an air bombardment of CASSINO town. Three med bomber groups followed by ten heavy bomber groups followed by three med bomber groups. Total approx 580 aircraft. First groups due over target at 0830 hrs, last group 1200 hrs.
   (c) <u>2 NZ Div</u> is to capture CASSINO and Pt. 193 (853213), thence exploiting SOUTH to open up Highway 6 and to the EAST and SE to clear the enemy between R. RAPIDO and R. GARI. This operation is being carried out by 6 NZ Bde. with two armd regts under command. Zero 1200 hrs 15 Mar.
   (d) <u>Plan of 6 NZ Bde.</u>
       (i) One armd regt leads followed by 2 inf bns. Start line northern outskirts of CASSINO. Rate of advance behind arty barrage 100 yards in 10 minutes.
       (ii) First objective:- incl Pt. 193 (853213) – Rd junc 854209 – Rd junc 860208. Codeword – QUISLING.
       (iii) Second objective :- Rd junc 853197 – inc 55 ring contour (8519) – R. GARI at 858192 – Stream junc 861197 – rly stn 8862201. Codeword – JOCKEY.

(e) <u>4 Ind. Div.</u> – is to hold firm existing FDLs with 7 Ind Inf Bde, and follow up 6 NZ Bde with 5 Ind Inf Bde.
(f) <u>Plan of attack of 5 Ind Inf Bde</u> – is to be in five phases:-
   (i) Phase 1 – Codeword HOMER. Relief of 6 NZ Bde on Pt. 193 and securing of Pt. 165 (852213) by 1/4 Essex.
  (ii) Phase 2 – Codeword HORACE. 1 Raj. Rif. to secure rd bend 850215 and area 851207.
 (iii) Phase 3 – Codeword HADRIAN. 1 Raj. Rif. to secure Pt. 202 (851206) and exploit to Pt. 435 (846206).
 (iv) Phase 4 – Codeword HERCULES. 1/9 G.R. to secure Pt. 435.
  (v) Phase 5 – Codeword HECTOR. 1/4 Essex after relief on Pt. 193 by 4 Raj Rif to secure MONASTERY HILL.
(g) <u>Arty</u>
   (i) Extensive CB programme throughout 'D' Day and subsequently.
  (ii) Attack by 6 NZ Bde to be supported by concentrations and barrage.
 (iii) Attack by 5 Ind Inf Bde to be supported by concentrations.
(h) <u>Air Sp.</u>
In addition to preliminary air bombardment, all available aircraft will be on call at NZ Corps throughout the operation.
(i) <u>Additional troops under comd 7 Ind Inf Bde</u>
'D' Coy 760 U.S. Tank Bn (Stuarts) and three SP 105mm guns are now under comd 7 Bde Recce Sqn.

INTENTION
3. 7 Ind Inf Bde will:-
(a) Hold firm on existing FDLs.
(b) Give fire sp to attacks by 6 NZ Bde and 5 Ind Inf Bde.
(c) Be prepared to exploit with infantry if enemy show signs of disrupting.
(d) Be prepared to exploit with tks toward Pt. 468 (832217) on 'D' plus 1 day if situation is favourable.

METHOD
4. <u>Holding of FDLs</u>
Existing positions will be held at all costs. In the event of an enemy counterattack against our sector, he will be destroyed.
5. Fire support to attacks by 6 NZ and 5 Ind Inf Bdes
(a) This will be carried out by 4/16 Punjab with 'D' Coy MG Raj Rif and one Pl 7 Bde MMG Coy under comd.

(b) Details as already arranged direct with comd 4/16 Punjab.
6. <u>Exploitation with infantry.</u>
In the event of enemy showing signs of breaking up on our front owing to events elsewhere 1/2 G.R. will hold in readiness one of their Res coys for exploitation role along western slope of Pt. 593 towards Pt. 569. This coy would only move under orders from this HQ.
7. <u>Exploitation with tks.</u>
   (a) Depending on success of attacks by 6 NZ Bde and 5 Ind Inf Bde, 7 Bde Recce Sqn with 'D' Coy 760 U.S. Tank Bn will move to lying up area along CAVENDISH rd. during night D/D plus 1.
   (b) 12 Fd Coy will then come in close sp of 7 Bde Recce Sqn.
   (c) 1 R. Sussex will hold in readiness one coy inf to move to area MADRAS CIRCUS. This coy may be required to follow up 7 Bde Recce Sqn in the event of a successful advance.
   (d) At first light on D plus 1 7 Bde Recce Sqn with elements of 12 Fd Coy will be prepared to move on axis CAVENDISH rd – ALBANET house (832216) to disrupt enemy in that area and on the slopes of Pt. 593 and to exploit SW towards MONASTERY HILL.
   (e) Further details later.
8. <u>Bombing</u>
All fwd troops will take cover in their present posns during the preliminary air bombardment.

Appendix 2

Revenge Force

RA   Lieutenant Colonel John F. Adye
RA Skylark   Major Scott Foster CBE, RA
Sigs Offr   2nd Lieutenant D. Fursher

'MACOL' Command

7 Ind Bde Recce Sqn:
   Major Malcolm Cruickshank MC, 2 GR – three Shermans, five M3A3 Stuart Recce tanks
   Captain T.F. England, 105 Battery RA

In close support:
   760th Tank Battalion
   Company D (Lieutenant Herman R. Crowder) – seventeen M5A1 Stuarts
   Assault Platoon, HQ Company (Lieutenant Victor F. Hipkiss) – three M7 105mm HMCs

'BARCOL' Command

C Sqn, 20 NZ Armd Regt:
   Major Pat Barton – sixteen M4A2 Shermans
   Captain Hooper – 166 Field Regiment in close support

Infantry:
   Company, 1 Royal Sussex (Major Dalton)
   Major Rankin, 166 Battery in close support
   Company, Madras S&M, IE Major Wheaton, IE

Appendix 3

Casualties by Unit

C Squadron, 20 NZ Armoured Regiment

Troop/Crew	Tank Fate
SHQ #15 Maj Pat Barton Tpr George Hanrahan (driver) Tpr T.W. Bell (co-driver) (DOW)	Bogged near Madras Circus but driven out
SHQ #16 Capt Pat Abbott	Left behind at Madras Circus
SHQ #17 Capt Jim Moodie Tpr Stillburn (gunner) Tpr Shorty H. Shorrock (loader) Tpr Digger Grant (driver) Tpr Baird (co-driver)	Set on fire but extinguished
SHQ #18 Sgt Maj Jock Laidlaw Col Gray (Indian Division)	Bogged – Madras Circus
9 Troop #3 2/Lt Jack Denham	
9 Troop #4 Sgt Owen Hughes	Had Lt Gray in his tank. Bogged – Madras Circus
9 Troop #5 Cpl Rex Miller Tpr Allan Colman Tpr Don Grant	Slipped off Cavendish Road at the bottom
10 Troop #6 2/Lt 'Buck' Renall (KIA) Tpr Frank Brice (gunner) Tpr Bill Rob (loader) Tpr Jack Blunden (driver) Tpr Geoff Blatchford (co-driver)	Hit by Panzerschreck in Albaneta basin, driven out

Troop/Crew	Tank Fate
10 Troop #7 Sgt Theo Dore	

10 Troop #8
  Cpl Dick Jones (Wounded)
  Tpr Steve Lewis (gunner) (Wounded)
  Tpr Tom Middleton (loader) (KIA)
  Tpr Jack Hodge (driver)
  Tpr Joe Costello (co-driver)
	Hit by Panzerschreck in Albaneta basin, driven out

11 Troop #9
  2/Lt Jack 'Stuffy' Hazlett (KIA)
  Tpr Geoff Townsend
  Tpr Frank O'Connell
  Tpr Bill Hastie
  Tpr Jim Wilkinson
	Bogged approaching Bottleneck, changed to Sgt's tank

11 Troop #10
  Sgt Alf Pedder (commander)
  Tpr Jack Dasler (gunner) (KIA)
  L/Cpl George Sorich (loader) (KIA)
  Tpr Bill Welch (driver)
  Tpr Leonard Gallagher (co-driver)
	Set on fire, hit by Panzerschreck by Albaneta House, restarted by Gallagher and driven out

11 Troop #11 Cpl Reg Lennie	Bogged near Albaneta House, crew rescued by Indians and Lt Chester M. Wright
12 Troop #12 2/Lt Bill de Lautour	Bogged near Phantom Ridge, transferred to Sgt's tank
12 Troop #13 Sgt?	
12 Troop #14 Cpl Basil Wilkinson	

7 Indian Brigade Recce Squadron

Casualties: 2 Shermans (1 recoverable); 2 Stuarts (disabled with mechanical problems); and Lieutenant Paterson (WIA, 19 March).

Company D, 760 US Tank Battalion

Platoon/Crew	Tank Fate
Coy HQ	
1/Lt Herman R. Crowder	Radio transmitter failure, transferred to Indian Recce tank
'Dead Eye Dick'	
? Pte John W. Sedicum	After Crews took over the tank, it was disabled by Kammerman's Panzerschreck on the track to the monastery. Sedicum and Crews held off the Germans for 45 minutes while the other crewmen were rescued by an Indian Recce tank and one commanded by Pfc Arthur Lehman and Pte Patrick Manning
1 Platoon	
2/Lt Chester M. Wright	Rescued some men from Lennie's tank. Tank became stuck below Bottleneck in Albaneta basin trying to rescue Reese's crew. Wright and one man from Reese's crew rescued by de Right
Tech5 Richard H. Selvidge (KIA*)	
Smokey Edwards (driver)	
Adrien Girouard (co-driver)	
1 Platoon, 1 Section	
S/Sgt John Kovak	Attempted to rescue two men from Custer's tank but forced to give up because of Germans nearby
Tech4 Melvin L. Edwards	
Pte George L. Tucker	
Pte Harold Hite (KIA)	Pfc Arthur Lehman and Pte Patrick Manning rescued two men from Hite's tank
1 Platoon, 2 Section, 'Devils Playmate'	
S/Sgt Lawrence R. Custer	Track blown off by mine then later destroyed by Eckel
Pte Wilbur Griffiths (gunner) (POW)	
Pte Doyle E. Cox (driver) (POW)	
Pte Floyd Snyder (co-driver)	
2 Platoon	
2/Lt James W. De Right	Rescued Wright
Tech4 J.C. Byrd (driver)	
	Threw a track by Phantom Ridge
3 Platoon	
2/Lt John A. Crews	Threw a track by Phantom Ridge

*Buried in Anzio-Nettuno cemetery.

Troop/Crew	Tank Fate
3 Platoon, 1 Section	
Sgt Leonard E. Reese (KIA)	Tank became stuck below Bottleneck in Albaneta basin
3 Platoon, 2 Section	Threw a track by Phantom Ridge
	Threw a track by Phantom Ridge

In addition:
    Tech5 Cletus H. Osweiler (POW, 19 March)
    Pte Robert W. Jester Jnr (KIA, 19 March, buried in Anzio-Nettuno cemetery)
    Pte Vurgel Munroe (KIA, 19 March)

Appendix 4

Citations and Awards

C Squadron, 20 Armoured Regiment

Leonard Patrick Gallagher, Trooper (70662) – Military Medal

Trooper Gallagher was the spare driver of the troop command's tank of No. 11 Troop during action of C Squadron at ALBANETA HOUSE on 19 March 1944. During the fighting around the house the tank caught fire at the rear. The troop command climbed out to attempt to put out the fire with an extinguisher but was killed by a sniper. The tank was then driven under the lee of the house where it received a hit by a 'bazooka' gun, the projectile penetrating just below the gun and starting a fresh fire in the turret, forcing the gunner and operator to evacuate. With the driver, Trooper Gallagher evacuated the tank through the escape hatch and sheltered under the tank. As soon as the fire had died down sufficiently, Trooper Gallagher climbed back into the driver's seat, tried the motors and found them still functioning. When the driver rejoined him it was found that the turret had been reversed and it was some time before Trooper Gallagher managed to switch the power traverse to 'full' so that he could get through to try to establish communication with the Squadron. He then found the wireless useless. He then got back into the spare driver's seat and, periscopes being replaced, the tank was driven out.

In helping to bring this tank out, Trooper Gallagher displayed courage and skill of the highest order in very difficult circumstances. Throughout he was subjected to intense mortar and shell fire with continuous sniping and MG fire. The going was very difficult as it was necessary to close the tank down completely owing to the shelling. The tank would undoubtedly have been lost but for his coolness and skill.

William Thomas Welch, Trooper (81318) – Mentioned in Dispatches

Trooper Welch was the driver of the Command tank of 11 Troop during the action of C Squadron at ALBANETA HOUSE on 19 March 1944. During the fighting around the house the tank caught fire at the rear and the troop command was killed while getting out to extinguish the fire. Trooper Welch then drove the tank under the lee of the house where the tank received a hit by a 'bazooka' gun, the projectile penetrating just below the gun and starting a fresh fire in the turret, forcing the gunner and operator to evacuate. With the fire extinguished, Trooper Welch and the spare driver proceeded to evacuate the tank through the escape hatch and sheltered under the tank. While the spare driver tried to function the engines after the fire had died down sufficiently, Trooper Welch drew the attention of another tank, which had come up, to the presence of a MG gun position in the house. The gun was promptly dealt with. Trooper Welch then returned to the tank. In company with the spare driver, he managed to get the tank fit to move and drove it out. In bringing the tank out Trooper Welch displayed great courage and skill of the highest order in very difficult circumstances as throughout the tank was subjected to intense mortar and shell fire, continuous sniping and MG fire. The task of bringing the tank out was rendered doubly difficult as it was necessary to be completely closed down owing to the shelling.

This tank would undoubtedly have been lost had it not been for the coolness and skill under severe fire of Trooper Welch.

Company D, 760 US Tank Battalion

Herman R. Crowder Jr, First Lieutenant – Silver Star (USA), Military Cross (UK)
For gallantry in action on 19 March 1944, near Cassino, Italy. While engaged in close combat with the enemy, Lieutenant Crowder left his command tank when the radio transmitter ceased functioning and under fire from snipers approximately 40 yards distant, went to an open-topped British reconnaissance tank equipped with radio to continue the direction of his company. He later went forward in this same vehicle under close-range machine-gun and small-arms fire to rescue the crew of a disabled tank. Throughout the entire action, Lieutenant Crowder skilfully controlled the movements of his company and by his cool manner and daring actions inspired his men to do their utmost. Home address: Yazoo City, Mississippi.

Richard H. Selvidge, Technician Fifth Grade – Silver Star (USA)
For gallantry in action on 19 March 1944 near Monte Cassino, Italy. As a volunteer on a rescue mission, Tech. 5 Selvidge accompanied his platoon leader in a light tank to evacuate three men from a disabled tank surrounded by enemy snipers and machine-gun positions. On their return toward the friendly line, the tank was disabled and they were forced to

abandon it. While assisting a wounded soldier to leave the tank, Tech. 5 Selvidge was wounded by small-arms fire, and since has been missing in action. His heroic assistance in evacuating a wounded fellow soldier typifies the finest tradition of the military service. Next of kin: Mrs Hattie R. Selvidge (mother), 1015 McFarland Avenue, Rossville, Georgia.

John A. Crews, 2nd Lieutenant – Bronze Star (USA), Military Cross (UK)
For exceptionally meritorious service in support of combat operations, near Cassino, Italy. On 19 March 1944 2nd Lt John Crews, Platoon Leader of the Third Platoon of Company D, was in an attack on the Albaneta House Area, Cassino. When his tank received a hit by an anti-tank projectile and was disabled, Lieutenant Crews ordered the driver and gunner to evacuate to a rescue tank while he and the assistant driver remained inside the disabled tank and manned the machine gun and 37mm gun. After he was evacuated to the Madras Circus Area he again went forward in another tank and removed the breech blocks from the 37mm guns in the tanks which had been abandoned because of thrown tracks. This was done at a time when there was a heavy small-arms fire in the immediate vicinity of the disabled tanks. Throughout the day Lieutenant Crews displayed his ability as a Platoon Leader and showed bravery under fire with complete disregard for his personal safety. Entered service from Chicago, Illinois.

John W. Seddicum, Private 1st Class – Bronze Star (USA)
For exceptionally meritorious service in support of combat operations on 19 March 1944 near Cassino, Italy. On the afternoon of 19 March, at about 1530 hours, the tank of which Pfc Seddicum was a crew member was put out of action by a direct hit from an armour-piercing projectile. The tank at the time was in an exposed position under heavy small-arms and artillery fire. When another tank came alongside his disabled tank to evacuate the crew members, Pfc Seddicum volunteered to remain in the tank and man the 30 caliber bow machine gun. He remained in the tank for more than 45 minutes during which time he fired approximately 1,500 rounds into nearby enemy positions. His cool manner and aggressiveness typify the finest traditions of the United States Army. Entered service from Lutherville, Maryland.

Lawrence R. Custer, Staff Sergeant – Bronze Star (USA), Military Medal (UK)
For heroic action in combat on 19 March 1944 near Monte Cassino, Italy. In the face of heavy enemy fire, S/Sgt Custer went forward in a light tank

to make an attack on Albaneta House. Upon successfully reaching his initial objective, he attacked on towards Monte Cassino to a point approximately 800 yards short of the monastery where his tank was disabled on a mine, and he was surrounded by enemy snipers. He directed fire on a German bivouac area a few hundred yards away and German troops along the road until the ammunition was exhausted. S/Sgt Custer remained in his tank until another tank succeeded in coming alongside to evacuate him to the rear. S/Sgt Custer's cool manner and aggressiveness typify the finest traditions of the United States Army. Home address: Battle Creek, Michigan.

James W. De Wright, 2nd Lieutenant – Citation
On 19 March 1944, near Cassino, Italy, Lieutenant De Wright took a light tank forward to evacuate wounded men from a disabled tank which had become immobilised by the rocky terrain. He volunteered to go on this rescue mission although the area which he had to traverse in order to reach the disabled tank was under heavy artillery, mortar and small-arms fire. By his courageous action Lieutenant De Wright succeeded in safely evacuating two members of the tank crew who had been wounded. The unhesitating risk of his own life in going to the aid of these two wounded fellow soldiers typifies the finest traditions of the United States Army. Entered service from Detroit, Michigan.

Chester M. Wright, First Lieutenant – Silver Star Medal (USA), Military Cross (UK)
Chester M. Wright, O-1011907, 1st Lieutenant, Infantry, Company D, 760th Tank Battalion, for gallantry in action on 19 March 1944 near Albaneta House in the vicinity of Cassino, Italy. On the morning of March 19th at 10:30 hours, Lieutenant Wright took the first section of his platoon forward in the face of heavy artillery and small-arms fire and evacuated four members of the crew of a tank which was stuck. At 14:30 hours the same day he led his platoon in an attack on the Albaneta House area in the face of heavy enemy fire. He continued his attack toward the objective until all possible further advance was blocked by another tank which had been knocked out of action. After returning from this forward area while under heavy artillery and small-arms fire, Lieutenant Wright again went forward more than 800 yards ahead of the friendly infantry line and made an attempt to evacuate men who were in knocked-out tanks. The manner in which Lieutenant Wright worked, without regard for his personal safety, was an inspiration to his men, greatly increasing the efficiency of

his platoon, and exemplifies the highest tradition of the Armed Forces. Entered the service from San Antonio, Texas.

14.(Panzerjäger-)Kompanie of Fallschirmjäger-Regiment 4
Raimund Eckel, Oberleutnant – Iron Cross, First Class; Panzervernichtungsabzeichen in Silber (Tank Destruction Badges in Silver)
For courage shown on 19 March in the destruction of Custer's tank he was awarded the Iron Cross First Class and at least one Tank Destruction Badge. The latter decoration was reserved for individuals who single-handedly destroyed an enemy tank with hand-held explosives such as a Panzerfaust, satchel charge or grenade. Post-war German accounts of the battle credit Eckel with destroying no fewer than three Allied tanks (but one of these was together with Oberjäger Wielun of the Pionier-Zug of the II.Bataillon, which may explain why he did not get a third Tank Destruction Badge for this).

Appendix 5

Galloway's Letter to Crowder*

                                          MAIN HQ 4 IND DIV

Dear Crowder   21 March 1944

I want to thank you and your company for the part you took in the Cavalry Ride to Albaneta.

    It was a great pity that the main operation didn't go according to plan and our infantry were not able to take the Monastery and join up with you.

    However, it was a very valuable diversion and a great effort on your part and a real contribution both because of the casualties you inflicted on the enemy and the fact that the possibility of the operation being repeated will undoubtedly prevent the enemy from thinning out there and so finding reserves for the main battles.

    Best of luck to you.

Yours sincerely,
Major Galloway, Major General, Commanding

* Pat Barton received the same letter.

Appendix 6

The Other Side of the Hill

Rudolf Böhmler, holding the rank of Oberst in command of I.Bataillon, Fallschirmjäger-Regiment 3, at Monte Cassino in 1944 wrote about the attack by tanks from Cavendish Road in his book *Monte Cassino*, first published in German in 1956 and in English in 1964, the translation carried out by Lieutenant Colonel R.H. Stevens. In the light of events that day, as described in this book, this extract makes interesting reading.

* * *

On the same day that the Germans had delivered these abortive attacks on Rocco Ianula, a company of the New Zealand 20 Armoured Regiment launched the attack that has already been mentioned against Massa Albaneta, up in the mountains. Towards midday a report had reached the battle headquarters of the 2nd Parachute Regiment of an enemy tank said to be approaching Massa Albaneta. The news was received with astonished incredulity, particularly at regimental headquarters, where it was regarded as a feeble joke. No one thought it possible for enemy armour to have penetrated into the steep, rugged, mountain country. But Major Grassmehl, who was officiating in command, knowing that all sorts of improbable things occur in war, sent Lieutenant Eckel, commanding the anti-tank company, to investigate.

Accompanied by one of his men and a war correspondent who happened to be there, Eckel set out. Carefully, making use of every scrap of available cover the three men advanced like stalkers towards Albaneta, 300 yards away. From the shelter of a rock they suddenly caught sight of a number of enemy tanks, rattling along a narrow mountain path. Eckel counted seventeen of them, Grants [not used in Italy] and Commandos [unknown model of tank] – sixteen tonners, that is, with one 3.7cm gun, a machine-gun and an anti-tank machine gun. It was obvious, too that they had been specially modified to enable them to operate in mountain country.

There could be no doubt about the object of the enterprise. These tanks were going to make a thrust at the abbey and try to relieve the hard-pressed Gurkhas on Height 435.

By this time, the advanced artillery observation posts had also observed this unusual attack and had telephoned to their batteries, and very quickly the first salvoes were bursting round the tanks. When the smoke cleared, six of the tanks were seen to have been immobilised. The rest were circling round the fortress-like Albaneta, firing wildly in all directions. Eckel and his companions crawled forward. From where they were he could not reach the tanks with his bazooka. They had to get closer ...

Calmly Kammermann took aim and pressed the trigger. Misfire! The second round was also a misfire. He now had only one round left; if that failed, the golden opportunity would be lost. But this time, the shot, well and truly aimed, hit the tank, which burst into flames.

Three of the tanks now turned in the direction of the monastery. On that course, Eckel rightly foresaw, they would be confined to a narrow hill path, the steep sides of which precluded any possibility of deviation. Eckel set off in pursuit. He had no short-range anti-tank weapon, but he hoped he might be able to lob a grenade into an open turret. But when his party were close to Albaneta, they found, quite by accident, three T-mines. That was indeed a find, and it did not take Eckel long to make up his mind how to use them. Hastening forward at their best speed on the flank of the tanks, the little party managed to get sufficiently ahead on the flank of them to enable them to plant the mines on the hill path. All unsuspecting the leading tank came on; from their cover all that Eckel and his men could see of it was the antennae of its wireless. Would it ... or wouldn't it?

Suddenly an ear-splitting explosion rent the air and a black cloud enveloped the tank. Eckel leapt to his feet with a yell of triumph. The trap had closed. The tracks of the leading tank had been blown to pieces, leaving it incapable of movement and blocking the way, for the other two could now neither go forwards towards the monastery nor back, since to reverse along the very narrow path was all but impossible.

The other tanks then tried to shift their crippled companion out of the way. The crew of the second tank leapt out, intending to fasten a tow-wire to the 'lame duck'. But they were at once caught in the well-directed fire of the paratroops, who had been watching events from the nearby hill-top. The crew of the crippled tank then went berserk and opened up a furious fire in all directions with everything they had. A few faithful mules, grazing peacefully on the fresh spring grass and oblivious to the evil intentions of the men around them, were the first victims.

Eckel wondered how he could put a stop to it. A hand grenade! And indeed, using a rifle grenade as a hand grenade, he succeeded in putting the tank's machine-gun out of action, but its other gun continued to fire furiously. Desperate situations demand drastic action. Eckel now had nothing left with which to continue the fight; but he knew that at battalion headquarters there was a dump of explosives. He dashed off at once, being hit on the way by a shell splinter, but 'his engine was still running' and on he went.

Breathless, he reached his destination, grabbed a few T-mines, some detonators and a length of fuse and ran back to give his booty the *coup de grâce*. With great skill he stalked his way nearer and nearer to the prey. To leap on the tank, tear open the turret and drop an already primed mine into the interior was the work of a moment. He leapt off and dived for cover, closely followed by two terror-stricken members of the tank's crew. Then with a sharp crack the tank burst asunder. The mine had blown it to pieces.

Eckel's exploit was too much for the watching paratroops above. The fever of the chase gripped them and they, too, wanted to be 'in on it'. Two of them, Wielun and Sack, managed to find some T-mines, worth their weight in gold at that moment, and rushed boldly at the other tanks and put two of them out of action exactly as Eckel had done. Hufnagel and Gudd accounted for two more apiece.

Twelve tanks were now out of action, six of them completely destroyed. The remaining five were still firing furiously, mostly at Albaneta, which they obviously took to be either a command post or a well-fortified strongpoint. Eckel now turned to the one nearest to him, stalking it like a hunter. The tank's entire attention was concentrated on Albaneta, and his approach was not noticed. He fixed a primed mine behind the turret and leapt for safety. Tank number thirteen had been accounted for.

The fourteenth was blown up in the same way by Eckel and Wielun working together. Panic now gripped the crews of the surviving tanks. Never in their lives had they seen anything like this. The devil himself must have been taking a hand in the game. Turrets were torn open, the crews poured out and sought safety in headlong flight. But they did not get very far. From all sides a murderous fire was opened on them; some fell at once, others tried to put up a fight, but they quickly realized the hopelessness of the position and surrendered.

Better safe than sorry, Eckel thought, and as twilight fell he called up a party of engineers from his own company to blow up the abandoned tanks. The tank hunt had lasted a good hour, and it had given the enemy a sharp reminder that to 'muck about' with the 4 Parachute Regiment, 'the tigers of Cassino', was a foolhardy thing to do.

Notes

Chapter 3: Operation Dickens
1. 2 NZ Div Operational Order No. 41, 23 February 1944.
2. 2 NZ Div Operational Instruction No. 21, 17 February 1944.
3. *Ibid*.
4. Blumenson, M., *Salerno to Cassino. The Mediterranean Theater of Operations* (Office of the Chief of Military History, United States Army, Washington DC, 1969), p. 434.
5. WAII 8/46 GOC War Diary Part IV, February 1944.

Chapter 4: Cavendish Road
1. WO 169/18780, 4 Indian Division RE War Diary, Appendix 5, Report on Roorkee Track.
2. WO 169/18780, 4 Indian Division RE War Diary, Appendix I, Cavendish Road; Appendix K, Report on the Construction of Cavendish Road, Part 1.
3. WO 169/18780, 4 Indian Division RE War Diary, Appendix I, Cavendish Road.
4. WAII Series 1 DA 447.26'66: Building Cavendish Road.
5. *Ibid*.
6. *Ibid*.
7. Walter Kerse interview, 15 June 2007.
8. *Ibid*.
9. WO 169/18780, 4 Indian Division RE War Diary, Appendix 5, Report on Roorkee Track.
10. WO 169/18776, 4th Indian Division Order, 'Revenge', 11 March 1944.
11. Headquarters, 760th Tank Battalion, APO 464, US Army, Operations in Italy, March 1944.
12. WO 204 and 275, 4 Indian Division Order, 'Revenge', 11 March 1944.

Chapter 5: Revenge Force
1. WO 169/18776, Appendix I, 4 Indian Division Report on REVENGE.
2. Headquarters, 760th Tank Battalion, APO 464, US Army, Operations in Italy, March 1944.

Chapter 6: The Token Texan Tankers
1. Krebs, John E. and Froeschle, Helmuth O., *To Rome and Beyond; Our Story of the 760th Tank Battalion, WWII* (Trafford Publishing, Bloomington, 1981), p. 2.
2. *Ibid*, p. 3.
3. *Ibid*, p. 15.
4. *Ibid*, p. 25.
5. *Ibid*, p. 34.
6. *Ibid*, p. 52.

7. *Ibid*, p. 55.
8. *Ibid*, p. 57.

Chapter 7: Tank Killers Turned Tank Men

1. Jim Moodie interview, 1999.
2. *Ibid*.
3. *Ibid*; Pringle, D.J.C. and Glue, W.A., *20 Battalion and Armoured Regiment* (War History Branch, Department of Internal Affairs, Wellington), pp. 235–6.
4. Theo Dore interview, 1998.
5. Pringle and Glue, *20 Battalion and Armoured Regiment*, p. 271.
6. *Ibid*, p. 275.
7. Theo Dore interview, 1998.
8. *Ibid*.
9. Plowman, Jeffrey. *Rampant Dragons, New Zealanders in Armour in World War II* (Kiwi Armour, Christchurch, 2002).
10. Theo Dore interview, 1998.

Chapter 8: Bradman Begins

1. Blumenson, *Salerno to Cassino*, pp. 438–9.
2. Molony, Brigadier C.J.C., *The Mediterranean and the Middle East, Volume V. British Official History of the Second World War* (HMSO, London, 1973), p. 784.

Chapter 9: Into the Mire

1. WAII 8/46 GOC War Diary Part IV, 1800hrs and 1950hrs, 16 March 1944.
2. *Ibid*, 2210hrs, 16 March 1944.
3. *Ibid*, 0820hrs, 17 March 1944.
4. *Ibid*, 0845hrs, 17 March 1944. [Note: Freyberg was clearly wrong about one thing here as 26 NZ Battalion had been committed on the evening of 15 March and was now preparing to attack the railway station.]
5. *Ibid*, 1335hrs, 17 March 1944.
6. *Ibid*, 1515hrs, 17 March 1944.
7. Phillips, N.C., *Italy. Volume I. The Sangro to Cassino* (War History Branch, Department of Internal Affairs, Wellington, 1957), pp. 299–300.
8. Blumenson, *Salerno to Cassino*, p. 444.
9. WAII 8/46 GOC War Diary Part IV, 1930hrs, 18 March 1944.

Chapter 10: A Change of Heart

1. Pringle and Glue, *20 Battalion and Armoured Regiment*, pp. 383–4.
2. Theo Dore interview, 1998.
3. WO 169/18851, 7 Indian Brigade Recce Squadron War Diary.
4. Headquarters, 760th Tank Battalion, APO 464, US Army, Operations in Italy, March 1944.
5. Krebs and Froeschle, *To Rome and Beyond*, p. 95.
6. WO 169/18776, Appendix I, 4 Indian Division Report on REVENGE.
7. Krebs and Froeschle, *To Rome and Beyond*, p. 96.
8. WO 169/18776, Appendix I, 4 Indian Division Report on REVENGE.
9. WAII Series 1 DA 50/10/43, Pat Barton – Cassino.

Chapter 11: Cavalry Ride to Albaneta

1. WO 169/18776, Appendix I, 4 Indian Division Report on REVENGE.
2. Rex Miller interview, 21 July 2002.
3. Allan Coleman letter, 2002.
4. Jim Moodie interview, 1999.
5. Len Gallagher, Diary 1, Tuesday, 21 March 1944.
6. Headquarters, 760th Tank Battalion, APO 464, US Army, Operations in Italy, March 1944.
7. Krebs and Froeschle, *To Rome and Beyond*, p. 94.
8. *Ibid.*
9. WAII Series 1 DA 50/10/43, Pat Barton – Cassino.
10. WAII Series 1 DA 50/10/43, Jack Denham – Cassino.
11. *Ibid.*
12. WO 169/18776, Appendix I, 4 Indian Division Report on REVENGE.
13. Headquarters, 760th Tank Battalion, APO 464, US Army, Operations in Italy, March 1944.
14. Jim Moodie interview, 1999.
15. Krebs and Froeschle, *To Rome and Beyond*, p. 95.
16. *Ibid.*
17. *Ibid.*
18. Pringle and Glue, *20 Battalion and Armoured Regiment*, pp. 389-90.
19. Theo Dore interview, 1998.
20. Pringle and Glue, *20 Battalion and Armoured Regiment*, pp. 389-90.
21. Len Gallagher, Diary 1, Tuesday, 21 March 1944.
22. Frank Brice letter, 2002.
23. Pringle and Glue, *20 Battalion and Armoured Regiment*, pp. 393–3.
24. WO 169/18776, 4 Indian Division GS Branch War Diary.
25. *Ibid.*
26. *Ibid.*
27. WAII Series 1 DA 50/10/43, Pat Barton – Cassino.
28. Len Gallagher, Diary 1, Tuesday, 21 March 1944.
29. *Ibid.*
30. Headquarters, 760th Tank Battalion, APO 464, US Army, Operations in Italy, March 1944.
31. WO 169/18776, 4 Indian Division GS Branch War Diary.
32. WAII 8/46 GOC War Diary Part IV, February 1944.
33. Bob Frettlohr interview.
34. Böhmler, Rudolf. *Monte Cassino* (Rupert, Darmstadt, 1955).
35. Headquarters, 760th Tank Battalion, APO 464, US Army, Operations in Italy, March 1944.
36. Krebs and Froeschle, *To Rome and Beyond*, p. 95.
37. Böhmler, *Monte Cassino*.
38. Werner Eggert letter.
39. Böhmler, *Monte Cassino*.
40. Headquarters, 760th Tank Battalion, APO 464, US Army, Operations in Italy, March 1944.
41. Krebs and Froeschle, *To Rome and Beyond*, p. 95.
42. *Ibid*, pp. 94–5.

43. *Ibid*, p. 106.
44. Böhmler, *Monte Cassino*.
45. Krebs and Froeschle, *To Rome and Beyond*, p. 95.
46. Headquarters, 760th Tank Battalion, APO 464, US Army, Operations in Italy, March 1944.
47. Jim Moodie interview, 1999.
48. WAII Series 1 DA 50/10/43, Pat Barton – Cassino.
49. Jim Moodie interview, 1999.

Chapter 12: Endgame

1. Jim Moodie interview, 1999,
2. Allan Coleman letter, 2002,
3. Rex Miller interview, 21 July 2002,
4. Cooke, P. *Warrior Craftsmen. Royal New Zealand Electrical and Mechanical Engineers, 1942–1996* (Defence of NZ Study Group, Wellington, 2017), p. 162.
5. Len Gallagher, Diary 1, 29 May 1944.
6. Len Gallagher, Diary 2, 1 July 1944.

Chapter 13: The Attack in Retrospect

1. WAII 8, Part II: Reports on the Battle of Cassino, Appendix 7 – Secret Reports on the Operations against Cassino by the NZ Corps.
2. WO 204/8221: Operations of 2 Polish Corps on Monte Cassino, May 1944, pp. 34–5.

Bibliography

Archives

Archives New Zealand, Wellington

WAII Series 1 DA 50/1/34–71: 20 NZ Armoured Regiment, October 1942–November 1945.
WAII Series 1 DA 50/10/43: Jack Denham – Cassino.
WAII Series 1 DA 50/10/43: Pat Barton – Cassino.
WAII Series 1 DA 50/15/2: Citations and Awards.
WAII Series 1 DA 447.26'66: Building Cavendish Road.
WAII Series DA 21.1/1/50: HQ 2 NZ Division G Branch Diary, February 1944.
WAII 8, Part II: Reports on the Battle of Cassino, Appendix 7 – Secret Reports on the Operations against Cassino by the NZ Corps.
WAII 8/46: GOC War Diary Part IV, September 1943–October 1944.

National Archives – Kew, London

WO 169/1386: 1/4 Essex Regiment War Diary, February–March 1944.
WO 169/18850: 4 Indian Division Operational Order, 15 March.
WO 169/18776: 4 Indian Division GS Branch War Diary.
WO 169/18776: Appendix I, 4 Indian Division Report on REVENGE.
WO 169/18776: 4th Indian Division Order 'Revenge', 11 March 1944.
WO 169/18851: 7 Indian Brigade Recce Squadron War Diary.
WO 204 and 275: 4 Indian Division Order Revenge, 11 March.
WO 169/18780: 4 Indian Division RE War Diary.
WO 169/18780: 4 Indian Division RE War Diary Appendix 5, Report on Roorkee Track.
WO 169/18780: 4 Indian Division RE War Diary, Appendix I, Cavendish Road.
WO 169/18780: 4 Indian Division RE War Diary Appendix K, Report on the Construction of Cavendish Road, Part 1.
WO 204/8221: Operations of 2 Polish Corps on Monte Cassino, May 1944.
WO 204/8222: Polish 2 Corps Operations, May 1944.

US National Archives

Headquarters, 760th Tank Battalion, APO 464, US Army, Operations in Italy, March 1944.

Personal Communications

Colman, Allan: Letter, 2002.
Gallagher, Len: Diary, 1 and 2.
Kerse, Walter: Interview, 15 June 2007.
Miller, Rex: Interview, 21 July 2002.

Books

Blumenson, M. *Salerno to Cassino. The Mediterranean Theatre of Operations* (Office of the Center of Military History Studies, United States Army, Washington DC, 1969).

Böhmler, Rudolf. *Monte Cassino* (Cassell & Company Ltd, London, 1964).

Cooke, P. *Warrior Craftsmen. Royal New Zealand Electrical and Mechanical Engineers, 1942–1996.* (Defence of NZ Study Group, Wellington, 2017).

Krebs, John E. and Froeschle Helmuth O. *To Rome and Beyond; Our Story of the 760th Tank Battalion, WWII* (Trafford Publishing, Bloomington, 1981).

Majdalany, F. *Cassino. Portrait of a Battle* (Longmans, 1957).

Martin, Colonel Thomas A. *The Essex Regiment 1929–1950* (The Essex Regiment Association, Brentwood, 1952).

Molony, Brigadier C.J.C. *British Official History of the Second World War. Volume V: The Mediterranean and the Middle East* (HMSO, London, 1973).

Phillips, N.C. *The Sangro to Cassino. Volume 1: Italy* (War History Branch, Department of Internal Affairs, Wellington, 1957).

Plowman, Jeffrey. *Rampant Dragons, New Zealanders in Armour in World War II* (John Douglas Publishing, Christchurch, 2014).

Plowman, Jeffrey and Rowe, Perry. The Battles for Cassino Then and Now (Battle of Britain International Ltd, Old Harlow, Essex, 2011).

Prasad, Bisheshwar. *The Campaign in Italy. Official History of the Indian Armed Forces in the Second World War 1939–45* (Combined Inter-services Historical Section, India & Pakistan, 1960).

Pringle, D.J.C. and Glue, W.A. *20 Battalion and Armoured Regiment* (War History Branch, Department of Internal Affairs, Wellington, 1957).

Stevens, Lieutenant Colonel G.R. *Fourth Indian Division* (McLaren & Son Ltd, Toronto, 1956).

Index

People and Places

Abbott, Captain Pat, 42, 51, 169
Adye, Lieutenant Colonel John, 84, 92, 93, 102, 116, 167
Albaneta Farm, 105
Albaneta House, 83, 84, 101, 161
Alexander, Field Marshal Sir Harold, 21, 22, 74
Allen Jr, Brigadier General Frank A., 22
Andrews, Captain George, 121
Anzio-Nettuno, 13, 14
Arunci Mountains, x, 13

Barbara Line, 10
Baron's Palace, 23
Barracks, 77
Barton, Major Pat, 2, 3, 42, 43, 51, 54, 55, 58, 60, 77, 79, 81, 82, 85, 87, 92, 95, 97, 102, 103, 116, 117, 167, 169
Bernhardt Line, 7, 10, 13
Biferno River, 10
Blatchford, Jeff, 2, 169
Blunden, Jack, 2, 169
Botanical Gardens, 70, 72
Bottleneck, 89, 96, 117, 146, 148, 149, 152
Brice, Trooper Frank, 2, 98, 169
Brooks, Lieutenant Percy, 82

Caira, 16, 25, 69, 80, 83, 133, 135
Cassino, ix, 3, 11, 13, 16–18, 22, 24, 38, 49, 63, 64, 72, 74, 81, 122, 127, 128, 133, 135, 159, 160, 163, 184
Castle Hill, 23, 24, 65, 72, 75, 79, 89
Cavendish Road, x, xi, 2, 25, 27, 28, 29, 31, *34*, *36*, 74, 80, 81, 89, 127, 128, 133, 135, 136, 137, 140, 145, 161, 165, 181

Chiesa & Monastica di San Scholastica, 65
Chiesa del Carmine (Convent), 65, 72, 73
Churchill, Winston, 7, 9
Clark, General Mark W., 10, 11, 18, 22, 24, 63, 69, 72, 73, 74
Coleman, Trooper Allan, 87, 119, 169
Coliseum, 73
Colle Maiola, 16, 17, 25, 31, 140, 146
Colle Sant'Angelo, xi, 17, 18
Cox, Doyle, 108, 171
Crews, Second Lieutenant John A., 89, 105, 106, 112, 117, 154, 156, 171, 175
Crowder, Lieutenant Herman R., 37, 80, 81, 89, 92, 104, 105, 107, 108, 167, 171, 174, 179
Cruickshank, Major Malcolm, 37, 39, 80, 81, 82, 84, 102, 116, 167
Custer, Sergeant Lawrence R., 105, 108, 112, 154, 156, 171, 175

Dasler, Trooper Jack, 83, 98, 103, 169
Death Gully, 97, 104
de Lautour, Second Lieutenant Bill, 82, *94*, 95, 103, 122 147, 170
De Wright, Second Lieutenant James W., 80, 89, 114, 116, 117, 171, 176
Dore, Sergeant Theo, 51, 53–6, 58, 59, 79, 170

Eckel, Oberleutnant Raimund, 105–8, 112, 177, 181–4
Edwards, Smokey, 80, 95, 96, 108
Eggert, Werner, 105
El Alamein, 54

Foggia, 8, 9, 10, 63
Frettlohr, Bob, 104, 153
Freyberg, Lieutenant General Bernard, x, xi, 18–24, 37, 56, 63, 69, 70, 72–6, 89, 101, 104, 122, 127, 130

Gallagher, Trooper Len, 83, 88, 98, 103, 122, 123, 130, 170, 173
Galloway, Major General Alexander, 2, 22, 37, 69, 73, 74, 76, 130, 179
Gaol, 16, 64, 70
Gari river, 7, 13, 14, 23, 24, 47, 48, 73, 161, 163
Garigliano river, 7, 10, 11, 13, 14
Grassmehl, Major Franz, 104, 105, 181
Griggs, Lieutenant Ron, 28
Gruenther, Major General Alfred M., 69
Gustav Line, x, xi, 7, 13, 16

Hangman's Hill, 23, 66, 69, 70, 72, 73, 74, 78, 83, 89, 101, 102, 128, 130
Hanson, Colonel Frederick, 28
Hazlett, Second Lieutenant Jack, 1, 51, 56, 57, 82, 91, 92, *92*, 97, 98, 100, 123, 124, 146, 147, 170
Higginson, Lieutenant Tom, 28, 35
Hipkiss, Lieutenant Victor F., 41, 80, 87, 90, 95, 167
Hite, Private Harold, 112, 112
Hornig, Captain Colin, 28, 37
Hotel des Roses, 23
Hotel Excelsior-Continental, 23, 64, 75, 76, 122
Hughes, Sergeant Owen, 85, 92, 146, 147, 169
Hummocks, the, 20

Jones, Corporal Dick, 96, 98, 100, 101, 170
Juin, Général Alphonse, 15

Kammermann, Gefreiter, 105, 107, 182
Kerse, Walter, 35
Kesselring, Generalfeldmarschall Albert, 9, 14, 130
Kippenberger, Brigadier Howard, 18
Krebs, Captain John E., 47–9

Laidlaw, Sergeant Major Jock, 43, 93, 95, 146, 169
Lehman, Private Arthur F., 112
Lennie, Corporal Reg, 98, 99, 103, 117, 149, 150, 170
Liri valley, x, 7, 11, 13, 14, 21, 23, 24, 47, 80, 128
Lucas, Major General John P., 14, 15

Madras Circus, 31, 36, 80, 81, 89, 95, 102, 103, 104, 117, 120–3, 130, 137, 139, 140, 144, 145, 146, 162, 165
Massa Albaneta, xi, 37, 76, 81, 96, 97, 98, 99, 101, 102, 105, 107, 116, 119, 121, 129, 149–54, 181
Matthews, Lieutenant C.J., 31
Mignano gap, 10
Miller, Corporal Rex, 87, *88*, 88, 119, 121, 135, 136, 169
Milne, Sergeant Frank, 28
Minqar Qaim, 51
Monastery, x, xi, 1, 18, 21, 24, 37, 69, 73, 74, 76, 80, 82, 101, 102, 116, 117, 121, 124, 125, 165
Monte Cairo, 79, 154, 162
Monte Cassino, ix, x, xi, 7, 13, 19, 21, 23, 24, 63, 122, 130, 161, 162, 181
Monte Castellone, 16, 28, 82, 137, 162, 163
Monte Trocchio, 7, 49
Montgomery, General Sir Bernard, 10
Moodie, Captain Jim, 2, 3, 43, 51, 52, 54, *82*, 82, 83, 88, 95, 96, 116, 117, 119, 120, 123, 153, 169
Morris, Sergeant Alan, 77, 78, 79
Murray, Lieutenant Arthur, 77, 78, 79
Mussolini, Beneto, 7

Newedal, Karl , 3, 105, 153
Nunnery, 65

Orsogna, 11, 58, 59

Parkinson, Major General 'Ike', 70, 72, 73, 75, 77, 122
Pedder, Sergeant Alf, 83, 88, 92, 170
Phantom House, 82, 89, 90, 91, 92, 117, 149

Phantom Ridge, 89, 93, 94, 95, 129, 130, 140, 146, 147, 149
Point 165, 66, 77, 89
Point 236, 72
Point 435, 23, 127, 182
Point 569, x, 150, 155
Point 593, x, 3, 17, 18, 69, 98, 101, 116, 129, 130, 150, 152, 156

Railway station, 18, 72, 73
Rapido river, 16, 18, 23, 24, 80, 159, 161, 163
Rapido valley, 63
Reese, Sergeant Leonard E., 114, 116, 150, 171
Renall, Lieutenant Harold ('Buck'), 1, 2, 82, 96, 97, 98, 100, 101, 169
Rob, Bill, 2, 169
Rocca Ianula, 23, 77
Rome, x, 7, 10, 13
Roorkee Road, 25
Roosevelt, Franklin D., 9
Round House, 18, 75
Route 6, 11, 23, 65, 69, 73, 76, 78
Ruweisat Ridge, 54, 55, 60

Salerno, 7, 8, 9
Sangro river, 10, 11, 57
Sant'Angelo in Theodice, 14, 24, 47
Selvidge, Technician 5th Grade Richard H., 116, 171, 174
von Senger und Etterlin, Fridolin, xi, 17
Snakeshead Ridge, x, 17, 18, 21, 25, 38, 69, 130, 140, 146, 147
Snyder, Floyd, 89, 108, 171
Sommerville, Slim, 79, 84
Sorich, Trooper George, 83, 98, 103, 170
Stalin, Josef, 9
Stenhouse, Lieutenant Colonel Edward, 25, 37

Taranto, 8
Tuker, Major General Francis, 18

Valle Pozzo Alvito, 25
Victor Line, 9
Volturno river, 9, 10

Welch, Trooper Bill, 83, 98, 103, 170, 173
Wright, Second Lieutenant Chester M., 80, 89, 104, 105, 114, 117, 150, 171, 176

Units

British Army units:
X Corps, 13
  46 Division, 14
Eighth Army, 10, 49
  New Zealand Corps, x, 18, 21, 22, 24, 101, 159, 160, 161, 163
    2 NZ Division, x, 11, 18, 21, 22, 51, 57, 77, 159, 160, 161, 163
      4 NZ Brigade, 55, 56
        20 NZ Battalion, 3, 51, 55, 56
      4 NZ Armoured Brigade, 24, 41, 57, 80
        18 NZ Armoured Regiment, 58
        19 NZ Armoured Regiment, 28, 65, 69, 72, 79
        20 NZ Armoured Regiment, 2, 42, 51, 55, 58, *78*, *88*, 119, 120, 140, 167, 169, 173, 181
          C Squadron, 2, 42, 51, 58, 59, *78*, *88*, 95, 119, 120, 127, 140, 167, 169, 173
      22 NZ Motor Battalion, 3, 130
      5 NZ Brigade, 23, 58, 74, 75, 76, 122
        21 Battalion, 24, 122
        28 Maori Battalion, 18, 22, 59, 76
      6 NZ Brigade, 22, 23, 56, 128, 163
        24 NZ Battalion, 67, 69, 73, 75
        25 NZ Battalion, 64, 69, 72, 75
        26 NZ Battalion, 67, 69, 72, 75
      26 NZ Field Company, 28
  4 Indian Division, 2, 21, 22, 25, 27, 31, 66, 73, 81, 84, 101, 160, 161, 164
    5 Indian Brigade, 18, 66, 80, 130, 164, 165
      1/4 Essex Regiment, 66, 89, 121
      1/9 Gurkha Rifles, 66, 102
      1/6 Rajputana Rifles, 66, 77

7 Brigade, 37, 81, 102, 104, 163
  7 Indian Brigade Reconnaissance
     Squadron, 39, 80, 87, 162, 165, 167
  1/2 Gurkha Rifles, 38
  1 Royal Sussex Regiment, 37, 95
  11 Brigade, 18, 25, 130
  4 Indian Field Company, 25, 31, 34, 77
  12 Indian Field Company, 25, 87
  21 Indian Field Company, 31, 34
78 Division, 18, 21, 22, 24, 25, 70, 72, 73, 74

US Army units:
Fifth Army, 10, 11, 22, 159
  36 (Texan) Division, 14, 47, 160
  34 Division, 16, 47
  1 Armored Division, 18, 21
    Combat Command B, 18, 21, 24, 80
    760 Tank Battalion, 37, 39, 40, 41, 45, 47, 48, 80, 82, 87, 91, 105, 165, 167, 174
     Company B, 47–9
     Company D, 37, 39, 40, 41, 80, 82, 87, 91, 105, 165, 167, 174

French Army units:
Corps Expéditionnaire Français, 15

German units:
Heeresgruppe C, 9
  Herman Göring Panzer Division, 14
  26. Panzer-Division, 13
  29. Panzergrenadier-Division, 14
  1. Fallschirmjäger-Division, 18
    Fallschirm-MG-Bataillon I, 76
    Fallschirmjäger-Regiment 4, 104, 156

NZ Phases and Objectives:
Bradman, 63, 160
Cobra, 24
Dickens, 22, 63, 161
Jockey, 23, 24, 72, 77, 128, 163
Joiner, 24
Libel, 24
Panther, 13, 14
Quisling, 23, 65, 73, 163
Revenge, 37, 72, 76, 80, 89, 101, 102, 104, 127, 128, 129, 162
Shingle, 13, 14